The Sandman
OBSERVATIONS FROM
A MOVING VEHICLE

The Sandman
OBSERVATIONS FROM A MOVING VEHICLE

(Sandy goes up the Coast)

Illustrations by Michael Bell

ABC
BOOKS

Published by ABC Books for the
AUSTRALIAN BROADCASTING CORPORATION
GPO Box 9994 Sydney NSW 2001

Copyright © text The Sandman 1998

Copyright © illustrations Michael Bell 1998

First published May 1998

National Library of Australia
Cataloguing-in-Publication entry
Sandman, 1956- .
Observations from a moving vehicle:
Sandman goes up the coast.

ISBN 0 7333 0579 2.

1. Australian Broadcasting Corporation. II. Title.
A823.3

Designed & typeset by Brash Design Pty Ltd
Illustrated by Michael Bell
Set in 9.5/15.5pt Goudy Sans Light
Separations by Finsbury, Adelaide
Printed and bound in Australia by
Australian Print Group, Maryborough, Victoria

2 4 5 3 1

The following 42,956 words are based on a journal
I kept on a holiday some years ago.
As usual, when reading my books it is better
to read aloud in a dull monotone voice.
Take your time too.
The slower you read the more intellectual
weight you give the story.

How the Journal Came About...

Sunday 15 December
(some years ago)

The thought of telling my folks that I was staying at Kathy Green's parents' hobby farm with Virginia and six others over Christmas was making me feel quite numb. I'd never been away on Christmas Day and I'd never been away with a woman before, so when I entered the kitchen on the morning of the 15th I was anxious. However, I knew the longer I left it the harder it would be for me to tell them. A stationary object gets covered in cobwebs, so to speak.

Normally both my parents would be at breakfast on a Sunday morning but for some reason my father had gone to work — probably to make some money. I only had my mother to confront and that was good because she was easier to tell things to. Nevertheless, I could still feel my father's presence: a light film of Holbrook's sauce covering a small plate, the smell of fried food lingering like gunpowder after a fireworks display, a depleted loaf of Tip Top bread hunched on the breakfast table like a wino begging for coins.

I sat down at the table. In front of me were four glistening slices of French toast stacked one on top of the other — a fried trophy, as my father often called it. I always have French toast on a Sunday morning. It's filling and yummy.

'Before I turn off the stove do you want any more French toast?' asked my mother in a robotic sort of way.

Normally I'd be quite gruff and say 'Yes all right' as if talking to her was painful, but on this morning I was bubbly and nice, like a young suburban shop assistant. 'No thanks ... I'm fine.' Naturally I'd have loved six pieces instead of four, but I declined the offer on account of I was being nice. I even made conversation.

'How many pieces did Dad eat this morning?'

'Fourteen,' she said.

'One day I'll beat him. One day I'll eat fifteen.'

Holbrooks

Most young boys felt it was significant when they beat their fathers in a footrace or an arm wrestle, but my father had cartilage trouble and could barely hobble so any victory in a running race would have been hollow. There was no point having an arm wrestle with him either. He could lift a dining-room chair with a toddler on it and I had weak flexible wrists. I needed to beat him at his own game — fried foods.

I soaked my second slice of French toast in the saucer of Holbrook's while I contemplated the best approach to take. Christ! I was nineteen, going away with a woman shouldn't be a problem. I'd been away before. I'd gone to Kiama with Nils at the end of Year 12. His mother even chased my car up the street pounding on the boot and yelling, 'My baby, my baby, get out of the car!' If I were Nils I'd be worried, but I had a job and I paid board. My mother interrupted my long train of thought. 'Have a nice time last night?'

'Yes!' I said.

'Where did you go again?' *(As if she didn't know.)*

'The Roma.'

'It's grubby there.'

'It's good.'

'You eat too much takeaway. All that fatty food.'

I wanted to say 'Oh that's rich' while holding a piece of French toast close to her face, but that wouldn't have helped. She'd tell me 'French toast is eggs, milk and butter and men need dairy products, not just women.' Then we'd have an argument about brittle bones and bandy legs. So I picked up my third piece of French toast and tilted it so the butter slid off like a reluctant yellow paratrooper. Anyone could see I was stalling.

Last night at the Roma Pizza Parlour when Kathy Green invited Nerida, Ross, Virginia and myself to her parents' hobby farm, I was happy. (Two other people I didn't know, called Rhys and Miranda, were also invited.) I was a couple sitting with other couples talking about couple's stuff. At one stage I laughed so hard I couldn't get enough air and I accidentally flicked Ross on the face with the back of my hand. I felt exhilarated, but my limbs were obviously not used to it. The only problem for me was we had to go there in the week before Christmas because Kathy's older sister Lyn would be using 'the shed' in the first week of January, which meant we'd be away on Christmas Day. The carrot for me to break with family tradition was the couples got to use three double beds in the shed. The singles, Miranda and Rhys, would have to go to the caravan park nearby. Only pre-established couples stayed in the shed — a harsh rule if you were single, but a juicy carrot for couples who still lived with their parents.

Virginia, Kathy and Nerida were old school friends doing Communications at uni. All three were eighteen. Ross, Shaun and I were the boyfriends — people thrown together because our partners were friends. Ross was 28 and losing his hair. He worked at TAFE and had very bad breath. Thankfully he was bland and didn't open his mouth much. Shaun (who was not at the Roma) was a private school-type with large black eyes and a *Dead Poet Society*-type haircut. He was twenty. I was nineteen and working as a cadet Real Estate man for a firm owned by a chap who resembled a well-dressed pigeon and a red-haired man who looked like Elvis. It was an unusual bunch of people to be going away on holiday together. A conglomerate rock. Lots of ill-fitting pebbles glued to a host rock, so to speak.

Kathy was the taste-maker in the group. Her parents allowed her total freedom from an early age, so she had the edge in life experiences and we always did what she said. Virginia told me when they were younger everyone hung at Kathy's because you could do anything you wanted there — smoke cane, heavy pet, play strip poker and swear. Kathy was strongly built, a tad earnest perhaps, but she had this unique style of dress and a high level of confidence. She always wore ripped second-hand clothing and carried an old tin bucket for a handbag. I found the bucket embarrassing and pretended not to know her when we were out together, especially in front of the Norfolks (the cool surfers who sat under the Norfolk pines). Every time the Norfolks saw Kath they called her a scrubber and spat into the bucket. In her defence, Kath appeared to enjoy these confrontations and she often gave as good as she got. As I got more used to the bucket I made an effort to walk closer, but you couldn't get too close or the bucket banged into your leg. That summed Kath up — strong, but if you got too close you got a bruise.

Nerida seemed younger than the others, like a Year 8 girl hiding love bites at fellowship camp. She looked the same age with her mousy hair parted in the middle, long nose and short bouncy torso, but she loved playing practical jokes — putting salt in sugar and placing berries in someone's nose while they were sleeping. And she talked about bonking all the time, like she'd just seen her first penis ten minutes ago. These qualities made her appear younger. Immaturity does that to people. I was relieved when Nerida told us that she needed to lie to her parents about the sleeping arrangements in the shed. I was contemplating whether or not to lie myself. My parents weren't strict Christians like hers, but they were possessive and frightened of losing me. It wouldn't be easy to tell them I was sleeping with someone. Nevertheless, I seemed more confident than Nerida. I was also glad someone was below me on the parental possessiveness hierarchy. If I was cornered I could turn to Nerida for support, or if I had to I could turn on Nerida — whichever came first. Actually, I hoped she'd have trouble getting permission and I'd look like a cool guy with groovy parents. That was all I wanted, to be a cool guy with groovy parents.

In the beginning I liked Nerida's boyfriend Ross because he was the eldest and I normally do everything I can to please adults. I also found his voice, which sounded like the Martian on the *Bugs Bunny Show*, very funny. However, by the sixth double date he was bugging me. He was deciduous — as you got to know him all his attractive bits dropped off. Sure he was well travelled and could talk about foreign affairs. He'd worked for ten years, saved heaps of money and taken long service leave. Sure he'd drive miles out of his way to pick up Nerida from netball. Impressive as all this was, everything Ross touched soon smelt of Pine O Cleen. He was a perfectionist and it irritated me. I just wanted to step in some mud, hop in his light brown Valiant and stomp all over his back seat. (Even that was covered in plastic.) They said he loved Nerida, but it was as if he was teaching her swimming safety, or helping her to get a boat

Humpo Bumpo

licence. He always told her what to do. 'Use the fish knife. No! The fish knife, the one on the right … fruit bat.' That was his pet name for her — fruit bat.

Of the three couples, Virginia and I were the newest. We'd only been going together for ten weeks, whereas Nerida and Ross were two years and Shaun and Kath were six months. I met Virginia at the beach when some mutual acquaintances and I played a game of humpo bumpo in a deep pool on the southern rocks. The girls got on the boys' shoulders then each couple tried to knock the other over. Virginia was on my shoulders mostly — the insides of her muscular thighs pressing on my thin neck, the backs of her almond-shaped calves kneading my smallish nipples, the crotch of her crochet bikini pressed onto the back of my hair. I wished we could've played at low tide because my mouth was often below the water-line and I had trouble breathing. I didn't want to ask her to get off because I was enjoying having her on my shoulders, but since I didn't know her very well I didn't want to say anything. I think my anxiety at not being able to breath properly left a strange impression. Underneath fun there's often panic and I think that's why it took such a long time for us to date.

Virginia is the sunniest person I've ever met, incapable of negative thought. She is athletic, tanned, with long curly hair bleached by sun and surf. She is also a 'touchy feely', in that she drapes herself over friends like a wet poncho. Whenever she meets someone (even for the first time), she hugs them as if they've just received extremely poor HSC results. I'll tap someone to make a point, like a bird pecking an injured lizard, but since I'm not a touchy feely-type person I don't fully understand it. I thought you only touched a person you were committed to. However, misunderstanding Virginia was good because it made me vulnerable and therefore more likeable. (Gullible people are always well liked.)

Everyone seemed gung ho about this holiday last night — everyone except Virginia that is. She took such a long while to come around to the idea that it worried me. Virginia was positive about every-thing immediately. Even a stain on a pale blue cushion was beautiful to her. I knew all the propellers powering our ten-week romance were not whirring like they did when we first kissed in front of the community hall ten weeks ago, but that's understandable. Instead of seeing each other every day, it was now every other day. That was natural too. Sure, some irritating habits that lust previously smoothed over were regularly popping to the surface like little parcels of evidence broken away from a muddy hiding place. For instance, when we watched TV instead of heavy petting (like we used to) Virginia was always doing something with her hands — making a patchwork jacket out of used ties or converting old Spanish wine bags into moccasins — and when I'd try to kiss her she'd make me wait until she'd finished the bit she was working on. It's odd being jealous of a moccasin, but surely it wasn't enough for us to lose our intensity over. Surely my impatience was not turning her off? There had to be another reason why she was less than enthusiastic about this holiday.

'Aren't you hungry this morning?' I hadn't realised I was staring at the slice of canary yellow toast balanced on my fingers. The longer you stop in front of an obstacle the more doubt you create.

'Eat!' barked my mother. Usually I put food in my mouth at a speed to rival a hummingbird's wings, but today this shed thing was preying on my mind. I had to say something, but it was risky and I don't like risks. When I'm anxious my right eyelid goes puffy. I got a tick in it once and ever since then it swells up whenever I'm anxious, or if there's a westerly wind. Nevertheless, I wanted to go on this holiday, and I wanted my parents to know about it too. So I had to take a risk. Even if it meant having a puffy eye for a few hours.

'Mum, I'm going up to Kathy Green's parents' hobby farm for eight days. Leaving next Saturday.' It just came out in one big lump, like I was a tube of toothpaste that someone pressed too hard.

After I blurted that out I waited for the hand of negativity to thwack me in the face. The parental thwack that always led to frustration, moroseness, bitterness, and finally the guilt that encouraged me to become too nice, which made my confidence rise so I'd ask for something out of reach. Like 'Can I go away on a holiday with Virginia for eight days?'

'With seven others,' I said, making sure she fully understood what I'd just said to her. 'Virginia, Nerida, Ross … you know, "the gang". We're all staying in a shed on her parents' hobby farm. Her parents will be there of course.'

There was a pause.

'You want to be careful of cyclones.'

Didn't she hear what I said? Virginia — going away — eight days, that includes Christmas Day.

'It's coming into cyclone season, you know.'

I couldn't believe it, no negative vibes at all, just some baloney about cyclones.

I didn't want my mother to see how excited I was so I gobbled down the remaining toast and shut myself in the bathroom to let out the smile I was holding back. I often share personal moments with a best friend and at this point of time the bathroom was my best friend. Unfortunately I hadn't envisaged the emotional stakes being raised and I didn't expect it would happen so quickly either.

I flushed the toilet, lit a match to burn off the methane (I always leave a metallic smell) and walked back into the hallway. My mother looked rather astonished to see me out of the toilet so quickly. Normally I spend twenty minutes in there because I play an imaginary football game using two pencils. I flick the pencils in front of my eyes to resemble legs running and provide a commentary in which my team always wins. However, due to bad timing my mother was in between me and my bedroom. I was trapped in our thin apricot hallway.

'Oh ... I forgot to tell you Aunty Coral's decided to make the trip up for Christmas.'

'So what!' I snapped, moving like a cat that didn't want to be patted.

'On Thursday I'm going up to her place to bring her back and then on Christmans Day all the relatives are coming over for lunch'.

I stopped listening because I suddenly realised what she meant by 'all the relatives' — it meant I was expected to be home on Christmas Day. I'd been thwacked, but I didn't realise it.

8.45 Sunday 15 December (A faithful re-creation of a phone call with Virginia.)

My father yelled out from the lounge room, 'Phone Sandy.' Why do I always get a phone call the moment I go to the toilet?

'Who is it?' I yelled.

'Virginia.'

Now I'll have a chafed bottom. When you have to rush you never wipe your bottom properly. But I didn't want to keep her waiting. After all, I had questions. I'd been round to her place twice and she wasn't home. I'd gone to the beach — she wasn't there. I'd phoned Kathy Green — she didn't know where Virginia was either. I was getting frantic. Early in a relationship you need to know exactly where your partner is all the time or you suspect the worst.

I picked up the phone. 'Hello.'

'Hi, babe.' (*She over-used the word babe.*)

'What's happening?' I said.

'Not much.'

'So ...' (*I squeezed out the 'so' to give the impression I was pissed off.*)

'Sorry about today, babe. Mum said you came over ...'

'Twice.'

'Sorry.'

'I couldn't have stayed long anyway.' (*I desperately wanted to ask her where she'd been, but I didn't want to sound possessive, so I acted disinterested.*) 'Did you have a good day then?'

'Interesting.'

'Did you go to the beach?'

'Yeah.'

'What time?'

'Eleven.'

'I was there at eleven.'

'I went for a walk.'

'Where?'

'Up the point.'

(Why did she go up to the point? That's where partners without accommodation went to 'dry root'. I changed the subject, but I kept the previous thought alive. It's not easy to do two things at once, especially when you're anxious.)

'It's great about going up to Kathy's, eh?'

'That's what I'm ringing about.'

'Can't you go now?'

'Yeah.'

'I thought you were going to say that you couldn't go, or that you didn't want to go.'

'I saw Danny.'

(Danny was her old boyfriend. I acted nonchalant because I didn't want to seem perturbed.)

'How was he?'

'What?'

(I was trying so hard to be nonchalant I must have mumbled.)

'I said, how was he?'

'Depressed.'

'Why?'

'Dunno.'

(I think she did but she wasn't saying.)

'Does he miss you?'

'Don't read something into the situation that's not there. You always do that.'

'Do I?'

'Yes.'

'Sorry.'

'I asked him to come up to the hobby farm.'

'Oh.'

'I hope you don't mind, babe.'

'Well...'

'It's not like that.'

'Like what?'

'Like us.'

(There was an unnerving pause.)

'I still feel affection for him, but it's not like us, you know. I've never seen him so down. I was worried. I thought, you know, he knows everyone, he helped Kath's dad lay the foundations for the shed and everything, and he wasn't doing anything and he'd never seen the shed finished, so ... It might be cool for him you know, chill him out. So why not, you know. I hope you don't mind, babe?'

'I don't mind.'

(Naturally I did mind, but I said I didn't because I never say what I mean. After all, I'm Australian.)

'You sure?'

'Would I say I didn't if I did?'

'Cool.'

'I don't mind at all.'

'So you said.'

'Ginny, I might come over.'

'I'm really tired, Sandy. So maybe not, babe. Is that all right?'

'Is Danny there?'

'Look, I'll tell Danny he can't come if you want me to. If you've got a problem I'll piss him off.'

'No.'

'Do you think I'm lying?'

'I just felt like coming over. I was just asking because if he was there I wouldn't come. Not because I was threatened, but because you already had a visitor and anyway I'm tired myself.'

'If he doesn't come it's cool you know.'

'I understand.'

'I gotta go babe, my sister wants to use the phone. Love ya, little man. See you tomorrow?'

'Do you want me to pick you up from Rita's?'

'Na. I'm meeting Nerida for a drink tomorrow. Miss you already, babe.'

'Me too.'

'Bye.'

'Last goodbye.'

'Bye.'

'Goodbye.'

Just what I needed, competition from bloody Danny Conners, ex-boyfriend, a Norfolk boy with shoulder-length blond hair, high cheekbones and a six pack stomach. I could see his game. Pretend you're down then ingratiate yourself via the romantically crushed door. The crushed for pleasure technique.

So Danny was a bit down. Big shit. But later, as I dwelt on the situation, going over and over the phone call, over and over our night at the Roma Pizza Parlour when we sat at one of the more sought-after tables under the throbbing neon sign that attracted drunks after the pubs shut, I began to realise I had the runs on the board. Virginia was with me and not Danny. Virginia had once said as much when we were lying on her lounge room floor with cushions over our faces. (I'm more truthful when I don't make eye contact.) She made it quite clear during one of her long muffled raves that Danny and her were through. 'I still feel affection for him, but not like that.' She even said that on the phone. Those were her exact words. I suddenly felt better.

I was writing thoughts for the next day (I often write quirky sayings in advance so it looks as if I'm good off the cuff) and I thought, 'I'm going to keep a journal of this trip.' It came to me out of the blue, probably because I was writing at the time. I just felt it might be interesting to keep a record of my private thoughts and observations during the holiday, especially now that Danny was coming. Years later, when Virginia and I were married, we could drag out the journal and have a good old giggle at what we were like when we went to the hobby farm.

I found an unused ledger I'd swiped from work and wrote the word Journal on the cover in Texta. I had a rough idea how to start a journal, so I wrote the day and date on the top left-hand side of the first page — Sunday 15 December. I decided I'd write in the journal before bed each night. It would be reflective and confessional yet also tell the story of the holiday. I promised myself I'd describe what happened each day and how I felt no matter how painful it was. Or how humiliating.

Sunday 15 December

'When two people want the same thing
usually one person misses out.'

I wrote that on the pad beside the phone while talking to Virginia and I thought it'd make a good first entry in my journal. Usually when I'm on the phone I write my name over and over in the same style, adding a scratchy shadow around each letter to make it stand out from the page more. But when she told me Danny was coming to the hobby farm with us I wrote that sentence instead. It feels good as a first sentence. When two people want the same thing usually one person misses out … Mmm. I like it. I like it a lot.

I had a feeling Danny was at Virginia's place while we were talking on the phone. She seemed restricted in her conversation, as if some-one was in the background listening to her. (It could have been her sister, I suppose.) Also, when I asked her if I could come over she said she was tired. Virginia is never tired. The idea of Danny Conners sipping weak tea from the same thin china cups I sipped weak tea from, sitting on the corner of her bed where I normally sat, or letting her plait his hair with the pipe cleaners she plaited my hair with, made me agitated. I knew I wouldn't sleep until I'd checked on them.

I didn't want to check, I knew it was wrong to check on them, but I had to check. I just had to.

I went downstairs. Mum and Dad were watching the movie *Weird Science* in which two young people create the perfect woman. Dad was sitting in the comfy chair with his legs spread. Mum was sitting on the floor, leaning back in between his legs getting her shoulders rubbed. I startled them because they both stopped doing what they were doing and looked up at me like two antelopes who'd smelt a lion. I told them I was going out for a drive and before they could ask me any questions I was gone.

It was about ten minutes to Virginia's place. I knew the route so well I didn't have to think about my driving at all. It was easy to be on the lookout for Danny's car. I knew if I saw his Holden Statesman going east down Garbutt Road he'd been at Virginia's. If he was driving west up Garbutt then he was on his way to Virginia's place. So I was half hoping to see him and half hoping not to see him.

By the time I got onto Garbutt Road I was anxious about what I might find. In the panic I decided if I saw Danny's car at Virginia's, or in the vicinity of Virginia's, I wouldn't go on this holiday. I'd pull the plug. Thankfully a few seconds later I changed my mind back again. After all, I'd only be punishing myself by not going. It'd be painful to watch Danny and Virginia together but it'd be unsettling for the others to watch me being upset. After you break up there's a period of two weeks where a dumped person can do anything he or she wants to without appearing obsessive or creepy. If I found Danny at Virginia's place I'd simply give back the ornamental silver horse she'd given me and I'd ask her not to wear the piece of leather from my belt, but I'd still go to the hobby farm.

Garbutt Road is long and steep. To date people who live at the top you really need a modern car, or you risk blowing a head gasket every Friday night. No buses go that high and it requires explosive calf muscles to ride a bike up there. Garbutt Road provides a natural selection process for the upper middle classes — only the better off can get high enough to date those who have the best prospects. The Gemini handled the steep inclines well provided I had the revs up. If I got caught behind a lower middle class-type in an older style vehicle (like myself), I wouldn't have the momentum to get up the last incline. If that happened, and it happened more than once too, I usually turned back and got my father to drive me. (He had a late model Holden.) The only problem with getting my father to help me was I couldn't stay very late because he had to pick me up before he got sleepy.

When you start up the first of the four inclines on Garbutt Road, the mountain range in the background blends into the night sky and all the houses along the top of the ridge look like distant planets. However, the higher you go the clearer the picture is. By the second incline those distant planets were simply two-storey houses on leafy quarter acre blocks — each incline was like adding a more powerful lens to a cheap suburban telescope. On this night, as I reached the crest of the third incline, the Gemini was really struggling. A car, obviously frustrated by my slow progress, came up close behind me and honked. I always feel guilty if I hold up traffic so to make up for any inconvenience I went as fast as I could down the other side of the hill, like a cockroach startled by a kitchen light. But no matter what I tried I could not shake this bloody tailgater off. I gave it the fast/slow treatment, something I'd picked up from watching my father drive, but that only made the car drive closer. I tried to wave it by. Nothing worked. I was under such pressure from this car I actually made it up the last incline without realising, but in the process I was forced a good kilometre past Virginia's place before I managed to turn into a side street and escape. Even then the back end of the Gemini spun out and for a few ugly seconds I thought I was going to roll. Then after I came to a halt it was even more bizarre because I'd stopped just in front of two boys aged about eleven sitting on mountain bikes. It was a weird situation

— me shaking with adrenalin staring at them, them dressed in expensive surf wear going 'Woah'. I wouldn't have impressed them like I did if I hadn't been pushed from behind.

I drove back and parked in the primary school across the road from Virginia's. I thought it might look suspicious if I just drove past her house staring out the passenger window. She might recognise the sound of my engine, or the neighbours would think I was an odd bod. So I parked in the school and walked down the footpath that joined up with Garbutt Road. It was an extremely hot night and the grass on either side of the path was full of creepy-crawlies, every little movement felt like an eye watching me. My heart was pounding, my knees were springing up high like a Spanish dancing horse and I was rapidly losing confidence in my plan.

Virginia's place was directly opposite where the path met the road. I stopped for a second or two before crossing, just to make sure there was no one watching me. These upper middle class-types certainly get a suburb quiet at night. The slightest sound or abnormality would disturb the peace up here. For instance, a twig snapping underfoot would make a dog several backyards away start barking. Satisfied that I was the only person watching me I darted across the bitumen and stepped inside one of the many oleander bushes that line Garbutt Road. An oleander is a good hiding place because you can see into it but you can't always make out who's inside it. At the base branches gather to form a natural step and I used this organic leverage to peer down the driveway, past the swimming pool where I'd pressed myself on Virginia. Much to my surprise/relief/dismay, Danny's car wasn't there. I even saw Virginia in the kitchen, sipping a cup of tea and staring out towards the coastal strip, like the troubled captain of a boat, but no Danny. I felt stupid. Especially when the two boys on mountain bikes appeared and asked me what I was doing standing inside the oleander bush.

Lights off at 12.15.

Monday 16 December

"The works" caramel malted

Kate, the woman who does the Property Management in my office and looks after the front desk during lunch was sick today, so I had to do her job — receptionist/property manager. Bummer! I'd planned to do what I always do on Mondays: go to Rita's Cafe for lunch. Virginia worked there every other day as a waitress, but she knocked off at two o'clock and I wouldn't be free until after two now. Not only did I enjoy my free hamburger and caramel malted milkshake, I loved being a regular. It's another advantage of being a boyfriend, or a girlfriend. Wherever your partner works you become a regular. When I walked into Rita's Cafe, Rita always said hello to me and because of that I instantly felt more comfortable than other people eating there. Unfortunately, today I was stuck behind the imitation wood counter in our dingy little office doing something unfamiliar. I find unfamiliar tiring. I prefer familiar. Normally I go out in the mornings with Mr Fewings (the red-haired man who looks like

Elvis) to list any new properties. I take photos for the display window, watch Mr Fewings complete the listing then write the copy to go under the photo when I get back to the office. Instead of being with Mr Fewings I collected rents, rang up landlords to ask if it was all right to send plumbers out to their properties and I answered phones.

I only got the job as cadet Real Estate man because my parents know the owner, Mr Wunderlich. I was offered a metallurgist's job, along with 40 other students who did poorly in the HSC, and I got down to the last three for a sales job with Comalco, but for the moment I was in Real Estate. I don't think Mr Wunderlich wanted to hire me. Every time I made a mistake he'd sit down beside me, roll his eyes, move about in his seat (like a bear itching its back), then he'd get up and leave without saying a word. An inability to talk to people is not a quality you associate with a Real Estate person.

Mr Wunderlich's about 50 with a pencil-thin moustache, a bird-like chest, spindly legs and a mane of silver hair that he always sweeps back with his fingers whenever he talks with women.

Actually, he did speak to me today. He told me to cut my fringe. He said it was too long for Real Estate. He reminded me about staff Christmas drinks on Friday and how it was important to look clean-cut in front of our clients. If I don't have a thick layer of hair over my eyes I don't feel comfortable — a long fringe makes a good hiding place. When thick wavy hair is viewed at close range it looks like tropical undergrowth. I often stare through mine and imagine I'm up the coast walking along a path lined with tropical vegetation.

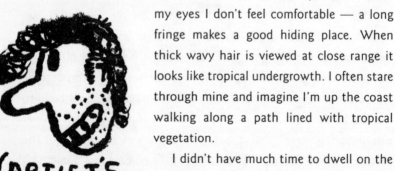

(ARTIST'S IMPRESSION)

I didn't have much time to dwell on the holiday, the staff drinks or a haircut. I was too busy thinking about how to get out of the office at lunch time. I needed to see Virginia, especially after our phone call last night. I needed to clear up my doubt before it became an obstacle. I also enjoyed getting out of the office and walking through the mall towards Rita's because it meant I could eavesdrop. I especially loved eavesdropping on shoppers frustrated by slow service. I loved being absorbed by their frustration, working out who they were and what they did for a living. I know I'm a bit obvious when I eavesdrop because I stare as well as listen, but we do our best work when we are most vulnerable. We just run a bigger risk of getting caught, that's all.

If I missed seeing Virginia today I would not see her till Wednesday, so I'd be wondering all day tomorrow what she was doing yesterday. Tuesday night was usually her drawing class and her father picked her up and dropped her home, but since TAFE was finished for the year I picked her up on Tuesdays. So now it was Mondays, Tuesdays, Wednesdays and Thursdays. However, neither her father nor myself was required because Virginia was going out with Nerida tonight. That was a bummer because I enjoyed the ritual of stopping at the milk bar to buy a Flake, a Cherry Ripe, or a Chokito and making her guess which chocolate I had behind my back. On the way home (after she'd guessed what chocolate I'd bought), we'd chat about our respective days and design the kids we might have — my eyes, your nose, my hair, your legs — or we'd bitch about her friends.

Why were Nerida and Virginia meeting tonight? Was it to talk about me? Danny? Danny and me? I also had to find a way to make her feel a little guilty about inviting Danny on the holiday without asking me first.

12.15 pm. It's amazing what a desperate person will come up with when they have to. As part of my Real Estate job I do this diploma course. Every Thursday afternoon I get off early to attend lectures. I went for the first two weeks, but I didn't understand anything, so I stopped going. It was all legal stuff — the Carbolic Smoke Company vs someone else. Everyone was older, they all knew each other and it made me feel as if I didn't belong. I cried the second time I had to go. The first time was a novelty, but by the second time I knew I didn't want to do Real Estate. So instead of going to classes I went to the Pizza Hut, where I discovered that I actually liked anchovies. In some ways the Pizza Hut proved to be far more educational than the Real Estate course. Anyway, the textbooks I'd ordered in the first week of term would have come in by now and even though I should've picked them up long before this I could truthfully say, 'My textbooks have arrived Mr Wunderlich and I have to go and pick them up.' When I finally told him about the books he made a series of grunting sounds then quickly retreated back into his office. (I think he meant yes.) Maybe I was better at Real Estate than I thought? Maybe he'd sacked me and I didn't realise it? Maybe he was a bear in a previous life?

1.05 pm. Having a real purpose made me walk through the mall at Olympic speed. Usually I rock lugubriously from side to side, like a battered schooner tacking into a stiff breeze, but when you have a reason to be somewhere you always get there faster. I raced up the escalator to the second floor of the arcade (where Rita's Cafe was), not even waiting for the momentum of the escalator to carry me along. Normally I stand still in the middle of escalators because I like stopping people in a hurry from passing me. Today was different. The closer I got to Virginia the faster I wanted to reduce the gap between us. I sprinted past the doughnut shop and its sugary perfume, past the bric-a-brac shop where the failed artist and his wife etched out a living selling oil paintings of horses frolicking in southerly busters, past the new shop that was replacing another new shop. The only time I stopped was when I got to the front of Rita's Cafe and I paused to push my eyebrows up with the tip of my finger to make my eyes look bigger.

'Hello, Sandy,' said Rita, carrying a tray laden with food towards the mezzanine level. 'How are we today?'

'Good thank you, Rita.'

'She's just gone to the Ladies.'

'Thanks, Rita.'

I grabbed a table close to the door so Virginia could see me the moment she returned. I watched Rita deliver some meals on the mezzanine level. Didn't those people know that when the sun comes in the window it's too hot up there? If they were regulars like me then they'd know not to sit in the mezzanine in December.

I liked Virginia's boss Rita — a divorcee with the ability to act cranky yet still be likeable. Every single working day Rita wore a pale blue dress, an apricot cardigan and a thick ring of mascara that circled her eyes like a Grand Prix circuit. She must have had seven dresses exactly the same because she always dressed the same way. I have four work shirts and each one is different. My fifth shirt can be any one of the previous four. Today my shirt was mauve. Tomorrow I might wear the lemon. Friday could be the mauve or lemon. Variety in work is essential.

A new waitress handed me a menu. Her face looked glazed, like it'd been painted on at a fete by a well-meaning parent. She didn't know that I was a regular and I never looked at the menu.

'I know what I'm having, thank you.'

'I'll get my pad,' she said.

I hoped Virginia got back before I had to explain to her that I was Virginia's boyfriend and I didn't read the menu, nor did I need my order taken by anyone but Virginia. Thankfully Virginia did return just as the new waitress arrived back with her pad. Once Virginia was with me I was a couple and that meant I was a regular and once I was a regular I felt more comfortable, and when I feel comfortable I find it easy to be arrogant. So I said to the new waitress with the glazed expression, 'Virginia will take care of me, thank you very much.'

Virginia and I kissed like relatives, then she moved off to start my burger. Normally she hugged me, holding me close for longer than was natural, but today she didn't. Why? I left my keys on the table and followed her to the counter to find out. I wasn't supposed to leave my seat because it's table service, but I was a regular and I felt I could do as I pleased.

(Faithful re-creation of our conversation.)

'Sorry about the phone call, babe,' said Virginia, not looking up from what she was doing.

'What?' (*As if I didn't know.*)

'Last night.'

'Oh.'

'It's cool?'

'Yes.'

'You're a babe, babe. Pineapple?'

'Yes.'

'Bacon?'

'Yes. Still meeting Nerida today?'

'What?'

'Nerida?'

'Oh yeah.'

(*Why did she hesitate when I asked her about Nerida?*)

'Where ya going?'

'Dunno.' (*There was a pause while Virginia turned around and placed the bun into the toaster and put my pineapple, onion and bacon on the griller.*) 'I rang back last night, but your dad said you'd gone out. I felt a bit bad about Danny.'

'A tenant had died in one of our apartments and I had to go and get the key and let the police in.'

'Far out. What did they die of?'

'Dunno.' (*I was supposed to be making her feel guilty, but she'd seized the initiative.*)

'Did you see the body?'

'Yeah.'

'Cool.'

'He just looked like he was sleeping.'

'Cool.' (*Rita walked between us. She didn't say anything, but the way she expelled an abnormal amount of air was a sure sign of disapproval.*) 'You free Thursday night, babe?'

'Why?'

'We're meeting about the trip. You know, who's taking a car, who's taking what food, who's sleeping where?'

'What time?'

'After work. At Kath's. Egg?'

'Yes.'

'Better go back to your seat. Rita gets the shits if I talk for too long.'

As I moved back to my table I thought, If it's that easy for me to lie about what I did last night, then it was also easy for her to lie about meeting with Nerida. We didn't talk much after that because she was too busy. However, whenever she passed me she let her arm brush mine on purpose and we both smiled at each other like it was a secret. That was gas.

6.30pm. Had rissoles for dinner. I prefer them with gravy rather than tomato sauce. (*NB Tell Mum gravy is better than tomato sauce on rissoles.*) No mention of the holiday. Instead my father and I had a long talk about the art of bending wood to make boats. Whenever he recalls the past his eyes water. I was happy to let him waffle on. I think the story about wood bending was an attempt to get me thinking about how things are passed on between the generations. Perhaps it was something to do with the imminent arrival of Aunty Coral? For some reason we always made a fuss when she was coming or going anywhere. Anyway, I purposely didn't pick up on what Dad was telling me. As long as I didn't have to talk about the holiday I'd listen to anything he was saying. I wonder if Mum has told him I am going away yet?

Virginia gets off work at 9.00. On the nights I pick her up I leave home at 8.30 to give myself time to buy a chocolate beforehand. Tonight there is no need for that. No need to preen myself, push my nose up with my finger to see what I look like with a button nose. So I filled in time creating doubt. Too much doubt creates anxiety, and anxiety makes you do things you don't want to do. I knew I shouldn't check on her, but I couldn't help myself.

8.35 pm. In a replica of the night before, I startled Mum and Dad in the lounge room. This time they were watching *La Cage aux Folles*. It was Dad's turn to get a massage. He prefers his feet, so he was lying across the lounge with his shoes and socks off while Mum was rubbing oil into his dry pale feet. As usual they seemed startled when I appeared, but before they could say anything I was gone again.

I parked the car a couple of streets away from Rita's Cafe and walked to the rear of the arcade, where there was a car park. All the husbands and boyfriends pick up their partners after the shops shut at 9.00, so there's a lot of activity. Usually it was only on Thursday nights, but near Christmas the shops stayed open late every night. I stayed in the shadows near the church next to the exit and waited. Five past nine; Virginia would be one more minute. I used the minute to peruse the car park for Danny's Holden Statesman. I was temporarily distracted by the fact there were more Fords than Holdens. By the time I'd looked over the car park, counting Fords and Holdens (Fords won), Virginia was standing at the automatic doors. She looked stunning. It was as if her charisma was making the doors open and shut. She had on a loose-fitting summery dress that made her thighs seem Olympian. They were the first thing that attracted me to her. Before I knew her well enough to touch them I used to fantasise about them being wrapped around my torso.

Virginia paused, then she smiled, like she'd seen someone very familiar. Her teeth were like a row of floodlights, her smile so radiant it could attract insects. I followed her eyeline to see who she was smiling and waving at. I saw Nerida's head above the roof of her mother's car, rather like an otter checking its territory for intruders. I was relieved Danny wasn't there, but I was also disappointed because now I had nothing to be morose about for the rest of the night. Virginia ran over to Nerida, then they hugged like lovers. I watched them drive past me. Unless Danny was lying down in the back seat there were definitely only the two people in the car. I felt stupid. Not as stupid as last night, but still stupid.

Lights off at 12.20 am.

Tuesday 17 December

Felt a little cranky today. Maybe because Mr Fewings was at a conference and I was stuck in the bloody office again. I'm sick of the bloody office. I'm sick of bloody Real Estate. I spent most of the morning in the bloody cubicle off the bloody reception area trying to imagine what the inside of the bloody shed was like. I had a vague idea of the outside from what the others had told me — a brick con-

struction on a sloping block of land — but I was unsure about the interior. I knew there were three double beds, but were there three separate rooms? Was there hot water? Was there a shower? Was there a shower curtain? Would I have to cook a meal?

The only meal I'd ever made was creme of oyster soup, and that was out of a can. If I hid the cans I might be able to pass it off as homemade. *(NB Buy three cans of oyster soup.)* I should find out the names of a few good wines too. Most established couples drink wine. *(NB Go to the bookshop and buy a book about wine.)*

I also wondered about the toilet. I'll drive miles to use my own toilet, or to use a toilet that is familiar. If the toilet in the shed is not private enough I'll have to drive into town and use the public toilets. What if town was a long drive? How would I react to Rhys and Miranda? How would I know if they liked me?

How do you know when someone is a friend? You know that you're friends when:

1 You've seen someone first thing in the morning.
2 You've made them angry/sad/disappointed and they still talk to you.
3 You've heard them fart.
4 You've given them flu or vice versa.
5 You've met both parents and you call them by their first names.
6 You can sit next to someone and not feel embarrassed because no one is talking.
7 You're forced to use a toilet straight after them or vice versa.
8 You've played the game Who would you rather have sex with? Who would you rather have sex with: Margaret Thatcher, John Major, or would you rather eat a dog turd?

If you experience four of the above you are friends.

I didn't get a chance to apply my test on anyone because I had to go out of the office in the afternoon. I had to take a couple of losers to see a flat. I hated that part of the job. Why couldn't they take their own car? If they don't take the flat the drive back to the office is excruciating. I get a couple of minutes' conversation out of the inappropriateness of a two-door car for Real Estate and then I ask them how long they've been looking for a place. But after that I run out of conversation. Unless they're talkative I have to drive with my arms pressed against my body to hide the two tropical lagoons that usually form under my arms from the anxiety caused by not knowing what to say to a couple of losers trapped in the back seat of my car. I suppose it was good practise for the trip. I may be in a car with two complete strangers, ie Rhys and Miranda. There was also a possibility Danny and I could be in the same car.

At least it was a nice dinner tonight — potato pie. Made a conscious effort to finish before Dad, but his teeth were making the chewing action before his plate hit the table, so he had a running start. I noticed he didn't drop his knife to pick up his bread either. He was able to keep eating and butter his bread at the same time. These little tricks were the reason why he was unbeaten at finishing a meal first.

11.30 pm. I wonder if Virginia is home yet? I thought about checking on her but I feel sleepy tonight.

Lights off at 11.50.

Wednesday 18 December

Mr Fewings

9.40 am. Drove Mr Fewings out to list a property located 'Where the mighty mountains met the mighty sea'. (I might use that for the display window.) Covering his unique teardrop-shaped body was a blue striped suit, a tight-fitting grey waistcoat, all capped off by his lush crop of coarse red hair brushed to look like Elvis Presley in the late1960s.

Mr Fewings is 55, but he looks older. He has an old-style feel, except for his hair — that belongs to a younger man. Mr Fewings has experienced two periods of rapid change in his life. One in the 1950s, reflected in his style of suit — the other in the mid-1960s, represented by his hairstyle. He's also resided in the local area all his life, so everything we passed along the way had some significance.

'That's where Louie hit a spill drain on his motorbike. Struck the ground head first and scraped his face completely off.' I pretended to listen to him but it's hard to make a personal history interesting when the buildings that reflect your past have been pulled down.

I didn't feel sorry for him because in Real Estate people thrive on progress. Mr Fewings was making a damn fine living out of ruining his past. Anyway, while he babbled on it took the pressure off me. Since we didn't have to talk I could think about other things — like myself.

11.35 am. We pulled into the long winding driveway that led down to the property we were listing. The sun had passed over the mountains and only a few isolated sunbeams lit the thick greenery surrounding the place. When you live on a dramatic cliff with stunning views of the coast you only get half as much sunshine as people in the western suburbs.

We descended a set of mossy sandstone stairs to the chatter of wagtails, red wattlebirds and magpies, plus the sound of running water competing with the pounding of the surf. This was the sort of paradise I imagined owning when I got married. I wondered why anyone would want to sell it. It was magical. I loved it. However, my impression of this paradise was altered somewhat when Mr Fewings knocked on the front door and a man wearing a sheer blue nightie appeared, followed by a gust of foul-smelling air so pungent it made us both wince and look at the ground.

Mr Fewings quickly gathered himself, smiled at the man and said 'Hello' (like a good Real Estate man should), but out of the side of his mouth he said, 'Peewee's nest, son. Mud on the outside, shit on the inside.' After a short pause he took a gulp of fresh air and like a police diver entering a muddy stream, he disappeared into the house to make his listing. I opted to stay outside and take pictures. It was better to be on the outside looking in than on the inside looking out.

When Mr Fewings reappeared fifteen minutes later he told me he'd never seen anything like it inside, and that's saying something because he's seen plenty in his 25 years in the game. Apparently the man in the nightie, once a noted barrister in the local area, had let himself go since his wife died in her sleep some years ago — newspapers all over the place, dirty plates piled up high. But the worse thing, and I almost dry-retched when he told me, were the flagons of urine scattered about the house. (Under beds, in the cupboards, in the laundry.) The really odd thing was that inside all this squalor the master bedroom was exactly how it had been on the night his wife died. Mr Fewings said that even a cup of tea the barrister's wife left half-finished before going to sleep the night she passed away was precisely where she'd left it. The vendor told Mr Fewings he'd never been back in that room again. You could tell Mr Fewings was thrown by this because as we were leaving I overheard him telling the vendor the interior of his house wouldn't be a big selling point. He usually lied about things like that.

All the way back in the car he waffled on and on about the barrister in the sheer blue nightie. 'I bet he's the sort of bloke who'll definitely know he's going, Sandy. He'll make himself a cuppa, go into the bedroom, lay down on the bed and go to sleep beside her. I'll bet ya twenty bucks.' Even if what Mr Fewings said was only half true, it was touching and a little out of character for him to be so emotional. Perhaps he was projecting himself into the story? After all, he did live alone and he was entering the heart attack years himself. Perhaps he was worried that the barrister might die and he would lose the listing to another agent?

I just made it to Rita's before Virginia knocked off and despite being very busy Virginia kissed me intensely. So intensely I was embarrassed. Even some of the other employees went 'Woah'. Maybe something happened last night and she was making up for it by being more passionate than usual? I like watching others being passionate but I can't handle it when people watch me do something private in public.

Finished my works hamburger and milkshake in record time. If I hadn't come from a family of fast eaters I wouldn't have been able to accompany her into the mall to wait for a bus with her. While we

waited I quizzed her about the rendezvous with Nerida, trying to trap her into saying 'Oh, I saw Danny last night.' But there was no mention of him, no hesitation when I asked her any questions about him. Drat! I told her about the listing Mr Fewings and I made in the morning. I felt it was going to be one of those anecdotes I'd be able to use for years. The image of the flagons of urine was a great way to finish a story — it lingers on like a person who can't say goodbye at a party. The half-finished cup of tea will be good too, but her bus arrived before I had a chance to tell her that one so I couldn't gauge its lingering power.

My Uncle Nev told me Georgie Fame (the English singer) never travelled with any luggage. He bought his clothes on arrival then left them behind when he'd finished his engagement. So with Georgie Fame in mind, I made a list of what I thought were the essential things I'd need for this holiday. I love making lists. I always use very neat writing with a little number next to each point. Funnily enough, I rarely get to point number ten and my handwriting seems to get messy after point four.

1 Tweezers: you never know when you might grow some unwanted hair.
2 Cigarette lighter: to burn off the methane after a pungent ablution.

3 A floral pillowslip: to cover overnight dribble stains.

4 Only pack enough clothes for three days. Clothes that haven't been seen for three days should be considered washed and can be reworn without question.

5 Take a few old files from the office and at the appropriate time pretend to work on them. (I thought I might get some sympathy if I looked occupied by my work. 'Look at poor old Sandy he just can't escape work.')

6 A few cans of creme of oyster soup.

I imagined that Danny would take a surfboard. I was sure Shaun surfed and since I like to be in the majority, I thought I should take my surfboard too. I hadn't surfed for six months, not since I stepped on a sea urchin and I got a sea ulcer. At the time, my take-offs were getting better, I nose-dived less, but I still couldn't go left. Facing out from a wave freaked me out.

9.06 pm. Picked Virginia up from work. Tonight was Flake night so I drove her the long way home because a Flake takes longer to consume than most other chocolates. As we motored along we chatted about the meeting at Kath's. I was relieved to hear Danny wouldn't be there. He was meeting some Norfolk boys at the pub. Something to do with someone's birthday.

'When did you speak to him last?' I asked, hoping she might stumble into the little trap I'd set.

'The other day,' she replied without vacillation.

'I thought you saw him last night?'

'No.'

I usually went to the pub on Thursday nights myself. All boys with partners did. Not to be at the pub on a Thursday meant you were under the thumb. Most girlfriends in the local area had

Thursday night jobs in the retail sector and between the hours of 6.00 and 9.00 pm 'boys with partners' had no commitments. So they went to the pub and pretended to be single. You could see their anxiety levels rise close to 9.00 pm because they knew their girlfriends had finished work and they'd be waiting for a lift home. The bravest boyfriend was the last to leave, but you knew the bravest boyfriend would be the one to get into the most trouble for leaving his partner waiting the longest in a dark car park. It must be unsettling for the bravest boyfriend to look around and suddenly realise you're standing in among a dozen half-drunk single men with no plans for the evening. This is where a fringe-dweller with no charisma had advantages. I could sneak off and no one noticed.

After making it up Garbutt Road without boiling, I was disappointed to find Virginia's mother Kay still awake and in a garrulous mood. She was attending to one of her many waif animals. People brought her injured animals and she nursed them back to health and then released them. So instead of Virginia and I sitting in the kitchen having tea and then going downstairs to brush each other's hair and kiss, we all sat together in the lounge room listening to Kay's Kris Kristofferson CD *The Silver Tongued Devil and I* while Kay bottle-fed a joey wrapped in a smelly blanket. We chatted about Samoa and how the whalers brought disease to an almost idyllic society. We also chatted about Virginia's dad Eric because he'd just returned from Samoa. It was as if Kay was drawing a parallel between the whalers and her ex-husband. I guess she was lonely. I was randy, so it was hard to think about anything but randy stuff. Kay didn't look like tiring either, and it was getting late. So as a way of kick-starting some action downstairs I said, 'I should go cos I gotta work tomorrow.' I knew that once I was downstairs I could open and shut the front door to give Kay the impression I'd left, then I could sneak back into Virginia's bedroom for some heavy petting. It worked a treat. We started off with two workman-like kisses on the bed. At first I was too aware of myself and I kissed rather poorly —

that was until she dabbed her finger in saliva and ran it around the rim of my nostrils like a professional water skier. After that I melted. In fact I got so hyped up I said to her, 'I've got stars in my eyes, Virginia. Stars.' The moment it came out of my mouth I thought, Oh no ... I shouldn't have said that. She's going to laugh at me. (I even saw her eyes go all watery.) But as I'm writing this now, thinking more closely about what happened, I believe she was crying, not laughing. I believe I said something (so vulnerable it hurt) that touched her emotionally. Well, it made her eyes go watery.

Lights off at 12.15 am.

Thursday 19 December

The first thing I noticed as I approached Kath's house was the front gate was wide open. I'm from a street where gates are always closed and the fences high. The only time you see into a neighbour's life is when there's an earth tremor early in the morning and everyone is forced onto the street in their pyjamas. And that's only happened once in my life. (It took me a few seconds to realise I had no pants on myself.) The second thing I noticed was Kath's stereo. The volume was loud, at what I'd call an arrogant level. In other words, you could tell from at least five houses away this was a premises that wanted to be noticed.

Virginia was already inside. I went back to the car to get a sloppy joe because I'm more comfortable in social situations when I've got something to hold on to — unoccupied hands drain the confidence. That's why some men can't relax unless they've got a drink in their hand and that's why I leave a sloppy joe in my car. If I'm ever thrust into an awkward social situation I simply go back to the car and get my sloppy joe. This particular situation was awkward for me because there were people inside I hadn't met, plus I was still dressed in my Real Estate clothes and I looked like a straighty one-eighty. Nevertheless, with my puce sloppy joe slung across my shoulder to give me a casual look, I entered Kath's shared house with more confidence than I would have had I done without it.

Inside was a long and dusty hallway that stretched out towards a kitchen where there was a shower with someone in it. I could see their silhouette behind a mossy shower curtain. On the wall next to the front door was a nail with a wet hanky hanging off it and a sign written above in black texta: 'For your own safety tie wet hanky around your face before proceeding.' I felt it was a joke. I almost knew it was, but I'd seen less debris in industrial run-off than what was in their seagrass matting, so I thought maybe the hanky was a necessary precaution. However, when I appeared in the lounge room wearing it round my face and Virginia and Kath saw me, I realised straightaway it was a joke. Lucky I had my sloppy joe with me because it kept my hands occupied while I pretended I knew the hanky was a joke all along. Kath said they used the hanky to deter any parents who visited unexpectedly.

...I realised straightaway it was a joke.

'We the first here?' I said, trying to change the subject.

'Miranda's in the shower.'

I didn't want to seem surprised that someone arrived early to have a shower but my facial expression obviously gave me away.

'She lives here,' said Kath, with a degree of exasperation.

'Sorry.'

'You don't have to apologise.'

'Sorry.' My second sorry was intentional. Virginia giggled, but not Kath. I've never made Kath laugh.

'Garlic curry? Garlic curry, Sandy?'

I said 'Sure' without really knowing what garlic curry was. All I knew was it was food and food meant chewing — my favourite hobby. Then Kath instantly skipped off towards the kitchen leaving Virginia and myself alone in the large multi-coloured lounge room. I felt very uncomfortable. My mouth was dry, my eyes were itchy, I felt like a new arrival at the Western Plains Zoo. One way to combat unfamiliarity is to seek out familiarity, so I sat down abnormally close to the most familiar thing in the room — Virginia. I guess it was odd to sit right next to her when there were so many other places I could have sat. However, the moment my bottom touched the oily cushions on the big green lounge Virginia said, 'Want a hand out there, babe?' Kath yelled 'Sure' and then Virginia left too. How quickly you go from comfortable to uncomfortable. There is only one thing faster than light and that is uncomfortableness.

It sure was a peculiar lounge room. The walls were covered with paintings that featured unsettling cat faces — cats on swings, bursting out of pants and so on. They were done in thick lumpy paint with big black borders around the figures. In the centre of the room was this long piece of plastic dangling from a light fitting, mysteriously tied into big chunky knots at regular intervals. Underneath sat a bucket full of water. You got the feeling something could crawl out of the water, climb up the plastic and leave through the hole in the ceiling. From the kitchen I could hear a shower and the sounds of suppressed laughter: talking-about-me-type laughter. Did they expect me to go out to the kitchen, or should I wait here? Unfamiliarity breeds anxiety. Anxiety clouds judgment, so I guess that would explain my decision to crawl down the hallway on all fours. I thought if I got closer and listened to what they were saying I could decide if I should go into the kitchen or retreat back to the lounge room and wait. Unfortunately, my decision to crawl down the hall coincided with the arrival of Nerida and Ross, and when they saw me down on all fours in the hallway I was sunk. But I didn't panic. Oh no. I simply rolled onto my back and acted like a dog. I knew from past experience it's best to be in control when you're caught in humiliating circumstances, that way it looks as if the humiliation is intentional and it makes those around you feel more comfortable. Virginia, Kath and Miranda, a dark Latino-looking woman wrapped in a small towel, must have heard the barking because they all stuck their heads around the corner to see what the fuss was. I suppose I looked odd kneeling down on the floor barking like a dog, but thankfully I didn't panic. Nerida, who could never stay silent for long, broke the eeriness by saying 'Cool', providing me with an opportunity to get off the floor and act casual. It had certainly been a bizarre start for me — sucked in by the wet hanky and caught out on all fours in the hall pretending to be a dog.

Shaun arrived late and drunk. As usual he had this way of passing off irresponsibility as charm. Three bottles of quality champagne helped. He wasn't in the room a minute before he was offering us all a glass of it and flicking his long black fringe off his handsome face like an experienced fly fisherman. No one mentioned that he was twenty minutes late. A private school education appears to provide you with a charming way of doing selfish things. (*NB Rhys, the only person I hadn't met, wouldn't arrive until after 10.00 pm. He was a barman and couldn't get off work until then.*)

How people behaved during the meeting:

* Shaun and Kathy were entwined on the lounge most of the time. Kathy had her legs across Shaun's lap and Shaun rubbed the top of her thighs with the palm of his hand. It was like the repetitive action of a windmill, up and down, up and down. The longer the meeting went on the higher his hand went.

* Ross had a stiff, colonial-style chair. (How appropriate.)

* Nerida sat in three chairs at once. Every time she made a point she stood up and flapped about and when she'd finished flapping she sat down wherever was closest. I'm sure she was an Italian man's arms in a previous life. Every time she felt a vibration she got excited and moved about.

* Virginia was slouched forward in a lounge chair.

* I was on a milk crate with a thin cushion on top.

* Miranda was spread out on a tan beanbag. Miranda is dark — black eyes, eyebrows, black hair cropped very short. She wore an earring, a navy blue singlet and a pair of denim shorts frayed at the edges. I'd say she's in her late twenties. She has a loud husky voice, a laugh that consists of three 'Ha ha ha's' and she calls everyone

'slags' all the time. 'Pass the chilli, slag,' and so on. I found myself glancing at her after I said anything just to see what her reaction to me was.

I had four helpings of the creamy brown curried gravy soaked in two large bosoms of white rice. The garlic in the curry was cooked for several hours and I was assured by Kath garlic is like a normal vegetable when it's cooked that long. To be honest, after two of Shaun's quality champagnes I didn't care what I was eating. I would've gladly eaten gravel. I ate fast too. I managed two helpings of the sauce before Ross even had his rice served up. It's good to finish first at something.

For the next hour we discussed the trip in detail. Nerida started off by announcing she was allowed to go. (I bet she had trouble keeping that under her lid.) I was upset to lose my only ally in the possessive parents stakes, but I was heartened when Ross said, 'Don't get too confident, fruit bat. Your old man could change his mind when he finds out there are no parents staying in the shed. You forgot to mention that ... remember?' Ross had a habit of smoothing over the creases Nerida's excitement made. He didn't like to look stupid and he didn't want Nerida to look stupid either. I didn't tell anyone about my Aunty Coral arriving and the prospect of me not being able to go away because of family commitments. I didn't care about appearing stupid, I just didn't want to be isolated. When you're isolated you look pathetic.

Kath gave each of us a map showing exactly where the hobby farm was. Up the Pacific Highway/past the Yamba turn-off/after the third bridge turn off at the Iluka sign/go past Woombah/just after the golf course there was a gate and that's it. She said it was about a seven-hour drive. Ross felt it was more like seven and a half hours and for six long minutes he told us why. When he spoke he made the same noise as a clothes drier. Shaun and Ross actually bet on how long the trip would take. I hope Shaun is right. I didn't like either of them that much but on my 'Who's my favourite person table' Ross was below Shaun:

1 Virginia

2 Nerida

3 Miranda*#

4 Kath

5 Shaun

6 Ross

7 Danny.

* *Bullet performer.*
# *Denotes first time on the chart.*

Rhys couldn't be ranked because I hadn't met him yet.

Ironically, the first four are women. I feel comfortable with women, but most of my life is spent craving the acceptance of men. I did better at school with women teachers. I was Top Ten material with Mrs McCann, but the following year with Mr Bartells I came second last and went down to the B's with Mr Rowe. Mr Rowe was one year away from retirement and he didn't care, so he used to bring toast into the classroom and talk about the Depression years. The smell of his toast, his dreary reminiscences, plus his lack of interest broke my spirit.

'Who's taking their car?'

Shaun was taking his car (a Datsun 120Y he drove at the speed of light) and he could take one person besides Kath. Miranda said she'd go with them. Ross was taking his tan Valiant, but he had a lot of stuff and could only fit one other person in besides Nerida. (Please not me. Please not me.) Kath suggested Rhys. Phew! I guess I'd have to take the Gemini, or go in Danny's car. I wanted to drive (a steering wheel gives you that bit of control), but in my heart I knew the Gemini would struggle to make it. If I went with Ross,

Danny would be with Virginia and I'd have to spend eight hours with the Martian from the *Bugs Bunny Show*.

Kath also pointed out that the couple's rule applied in the shed, so Rhys, Miranda and Danny had to stay at the caravan park. There was a hesitation when she said 'Danny' and I didn't like the glances everyone exchanged after she'd said it, but I was in and Danny was out. It was official. I also found it comforting that Miranda was the only person present not in the 'club'. Kath said as much. 'Who's not in the club then, slag?' To which Miranda replied, 'What if I get lucky, can I get to stay in the shed then, slag?'

'Only if one of us break up,' said Shaun.

Then Kath took the floor again and rattled on, like she was reading from a dry pamphlet about the Gold Coast hinterland. 'In the shed there are three beds: two queens, one double. Shaun and I are in one queen, Ross and Nerida get the other—and you (Virginia and I) get the double. It's squeaky, so everyone will know what you're doing.'

'Are we in the same room?' said Nerida, doing her best impression of fizz bursting out of an almost opened champagne bottle.

'There's a partition,' replied Kath.

Nerida jumped onto my lap and put her arms around me and pretended to kiss my cheeks. 'Let's swap one night. Come on. Let's swap.' Everyone went 'Woah'. (Except Ross.) I didn't want to swap, but I went 'Woah'. After all I was in the club now, so I had to act like a club member. Ross didn't even try. He shits me.

Everyone had to cook a meal. Here's a list of what people are cooking:

Shaun:	rack of lamb
Virginia:	Greek chicken
Ross:	baked dinner
Nerida:	spinach pie
Kath:	felafels
Sandy:	creme of oyster soup.

Shaun said he'd buy wine and we could put in the money later. He made a point of telling Ross he wouldn't be purchasing any of those sweet German wines he liked. Ross bristled, as he did with any comment that appeared critical of him. I don't drink wine myself but I was happy to put money in if it bugged Ross. Sometimes I just feel like getting Ross's skin and pinching it until it turns into a yellow bruise. I know it sounds as if I've got it in for him but he brings out that side of me. What does Nerida see in him? She's much more attractive than him.

Kath mentioned that no one should give presents on Christmas Day either. Instead we'd give ourselves in the form of an eisteddfod. Each person would perform a piece that revealed something about their personality — a sketch, a song, a dance and so on. Everyone was expected to participate. I hadn't done a lot of performing, but I was drawn to limelight. It felt natural for me to be in it. I'd played a kangaroo in Year 9 — I hopped on stage and was killed by white explorers while drinking at a cellophane billabong and at our Year 12 break-up assembly I imitated our Science Master, who, for some reason that escapes me now, squashed a banana in his face. I loved both the experiences.

The final part of the night was unusual. After the arrangements were discussed Kath turned off the lights and lit the bottom of the plastic tail suspended from the light fitting. The plastic knots instantly formed bluey-red fireballs before they turned into liquid and dripped one by one into the bucket of water, making an eerie whirring sound, followed by a plop and a hiss when they hit the water. Kath said each knot represented the eight travellers and their journey north. It was a bit hippie for my liking and the pungent fumes created by the burning plastic made it seem as if someone had started up a defective lawn mower inside the house. I said to Kath (and I wished I hadn't), 'Since our trip is north I bet you'd have liked the flames to have burnt upwards eh.' I didn't say it with any assurance, so I didn't get much of a laugh. In fact I got no laughs.

We all agreed to meet at Kath's place at 5.00 am on Saturday morning, then leave in a convoy stopping for lunch when we arrived at the Big Banana. I still didn't know whose car I was in (mine or his), but it seemed as if I'd be in a car with Danny and Virginia.

(NB I finally met Rhys as we were leaving. He was tall and thin with a shaven head. He wore a shiny green polka dot shirt, brown slim fit jeans and eyeliner. I'd imagined him as a stocky Welsh rugby union player.)

'This is Sandy,' said Virginia.

'Hello, Sandy.'

'Hello.' *There was an awkward pause. A lot of things to say flashed past me, like debris in a swollen river, but the only thing I could pluck out in a hurry was:* 'Is Rhys a Welsh name?'

'No darling, it's poof.'

(I acted cool by looking down and picking my teeth. It always helps when you're a little embarrassed to act coy.)

'Sorry I'm late, darling,' he said, looking at me but including the others. 'Did I miss anything important?'

'Everything,' said Miranda.

'Good.'

'Slut.'

'Slag.'

Then Rhys walked off down the hallway where he kissed Shaun (who was lingering in the lounge) full on the lips.

(Faithful re-creation of trip home.)

On the way home Virginia was quiet, so I asked her if anything was wrong.

'No.'

(Silence.)

'Does Rhys live at Kath's house?'

'Yes.'

(Silence.)

'Should I kiss him when we greet?' I didn't mean to ask that. I was just thinking it. This is a problem for the only child, you forget there's another world outside your own rich inner life. I wondered if this was the end. It felt like the end. Please don't let it be the end.

Lights off at 11.45.

Got back up at 12.30. I couldn't sleep. I had a big bowl of ice cream with strawberry sauce and that seemed to help.

Lights off at 1.05.

Friday 20 December

It's after midnight. I'm shaky. Can't sleep.
Something odd happened at the staff
Christmas drinks and it's going to
affect the holiday. I just know it.

I'd never been to a staff
Christmas drinks before. I thought
it would be Mr Wunderlich, Mr
Fewings, Theo Papadopolous (our
sales rep), Kate and me talking shop for
a few hours, but about 50 people crammed
into our little Real Estate cave. Some of our biggest clients were
there too, plus bank managers, insurance people, other agents and
assorted people we could use at a later date for personal gain. A
mixture of alcohol, Mr Wunderlich's personal recordings of steam
organ music and the sound of seedy middle-aged men laughing
made our brown office at the dead end of town feel like an illegal
casino. At least the one illegal casino I'd been in.

I was under instructions to make sure everyone had a drink. That
was my brief: keep people happy. So for two hours I served beer,
champagne, wine and pre-mixed Margarita's. However, by five o'clock
people were helping themselves (me too) and I was free to do as I
pleased. Everybody was in good spirits. Mr Wunderlich was literally
beaming, his sinewy fingers kneading his mane of thick silvery hair
like a hirsute Chopin whenever he talked to a woman. Mr Fewings
had a young bank manager pinned against a wall, telling him loudly,
'You're a top fuckin' bloke Gracey,' his face literally boiling over with
alcohol. Kate was animated and warm, laughing so hard at people's
impressions of fellow agents I thought she'd blow her clothes off.

Theo was suspiciously hunched inside a group of insurance folk, his big black eyes darting about like a small bird trying to decide if it should take a drink or not. My colleagues appeared like strangers.

I'd harmlessly attached myself to the fringes of a large group at the dark end of the office. Mainly agents from other companies. I laughed when they laughed, swore when,it seemed appropriate. I was there — nothing more, nothing less. But that changed when one agent, a woman in her late thirties called Terri, started paying me a lot of attention; touching my arm, asking my opinion about things, staring at me for no reason. I couldn't work it out. Perhaps I was too quiet — you know, a closed door creates interest and all that?

Terri had a soft round face, a hairstyle just short of an Afro and because her eyes closed at the end of each sentence she had this alluring sleepy quality. But why me? There were more attractive men in the room than me. Her attention made me nervous, but because it was so flattering I stayed put and absorbed it like a brand new sponge. After twenty minutes the group, sensing something private between Terri and myself, cut us loose, or more specifically, left us alone in the corner of the dimly lit office. Being alone with Terri was exciting yet awkward, exhilarating yet scary, fun but terrifying. I mainly listened because I had nothing witty to say, but when we started telling each other about ourselves I fared better. Myself is something I know about. The longer the conversation went on the more attractive I felt, the more confident I was and the further up the river of darkness I drifted. I also noticed from the corner of my good eye (my right eye was injured by a fire cracker), that people were watching me. Every time I caught Theo's eye he raised his eyebrows and winked. I had to be careful here. My colleagues knew I had a girlfriend, any 'move' on Terri would be seen as cheating.

The situation turned more serious when Terri had to go to the toilet and before she left she kissed me on the cheek using her eyelashes (it felt like a fly crawling on my face).

'Wait here,' she said. 'You're mine.' We were standing no more than two centimetres apart. I was breathing so heavily through my nose I moved a strand of hair on her face up and down. I hoped nasal air didn't smell. After she left I tried to check it by cupping my hand under my nose and breathing out. My test was inconclusive. I decided the moment she returned from the toilet I'd come straight out with it and say, 'Look Terri, I'm in a relationship.' I had to be fair on Virginia. I loved Virginia. No one could ever replace her. I looked around the office, everybody was staring at me. (Where's a sloppy joe when I need it?) Theo called me over.

'No, she told me to wait here,' I mouthed back to him.

He came over to me instead. 'Sandy.'

'What?'

'Terri eh?'

'What?'

'She wants you, mate.'

I was too embarrassed to speak, so I coughed.

'What're ya going to do about it?'

'I don't know.'

'Go for it,' he said as he tiptoed back to his group.

What if I said 'I'm taken' and Terri said, 'Do you think this is a come on?' That would be uncomfortable. What if she was just being friendly towards me? I picked up a drink to occupy my hands and used the moment to check myself out, like a beaver sizing up a log. What would I think of me if I saw me at a party? Squat? Cuddly? Wooden? I decided to play a game — flaws vs positive features. A mark to me for each positive feature, a mark to my flaws for each negative one. **Hair:** raven black spinnaker — 1–0 Sandy. **Eyebrows:** thick and strong — 2–0 Sandman. **Eyes:** big round cow eyes with lovely long lashes — 3–0

Sandman. **Nose:** sharp and angular — 3–1 Sandy. **Lips:** thin and prone to mouth scum — 3–2 Sandy. **Arms:** if you put ice cream and custard on them they'd be a dessert — 3 all. **Chest:** lower than stomach and very hairy — 4–3 Flaws. **Stomach:** round and firm, like an upturned pyrex bowl — 5–3 Flaws. **Penis:** — 6–3 Flaws. **Legs:** hairy, but calves have a nice almond shape — 6–4 Flaws. **Feet:** flat and wide like two pieces of gravy beef — 7–4 Flaws. Flaws win 7–4.

Terri returned and nudged in beside me, like a long-term partner sliding into a comfortable double bed. The unfamiliarity of her touch made the hairs on the back of my neck stand up and the floorboards around my groin creak. Her hand was soft and cool. Mine was sweating so much salmon would soon start swimming up my forearm to lay their eggs. Why do you have to sweat when you're anxious? Then Terri whispered, 'I'm going to meet some friends at a wine bar. Do you want to come with me?' I acted nonchalant, but my nose was literally whistling because the kettle below was boiling. It's damn hard to conceal excitement / doubts / eagerness / willingness and guilt all at the same time. I searched for an excuse not to go with her.

'I have to stay and help clean up.' *(Pathetic!)*

'Oh come on, swarthy. Come to the wine bar.'

'Okay.'

Terri towed me around with her as we said our goodbyes, like the bride and groom at a passionless wedding. There weren't many people left at the party and those who were left had the wobbly boot on. We stopped in front of Mr Fewings. He looked at me as if he was watching Peruvian television and the reception was bad. He was so drunk he wasn't sure who I was, or what channel he was receiving me on. I'm sure he only shook my hand because he thought I was a client of his. 'Good on ya, shag.' Even though he was about to slide down the wall and collapse onto the floor his Real Estate muscles were still flexing. 'Here, take my card pal.' Terri and I finished our goodbyes with Mr Wunderlich. Much to my surprise he embraced me like a son, wished me a Merry Christmas as if he really meant it, then he turned around and went straight back to talking with a tall woman in a pants suit, his fingers twirling his grey mane like a drum major. I'd never seen him so happy.

At this point I thought I'd ring home and tell Mum I was still at work and could she put my dinner in the oven. Friday was steak and onion gravy night. A big one to miss out on. But before I dialled I realised Aunty Coral would be there and I was supposed to be there as well. When an only child doesn't turn up to an important family function it's glaringly obvious. I'd already let the family down when I told Mum I'd get off work early and pick Aunty Coral up from the airport, knowing full well it was staff drinks today and I wouldn't be able to. I wanted to appear family orientated. I truly did. But something always stopped me — probably my family. I was in the clear though because the moment I got to work I phoned my mother and told her that Mr Wunderlich wouldn't let me off early. I made him seem like the culprit.

The wine bar Terri mentioned was called Tilly's and it was located across town. I'd never been there, but I knew of it. It was an over-30s singles bar. I believe we got a cab, but we may have sailed. Tilly's was as you'd expect it to be — a wooden place built to look like a keg. The entrance was designed to resemble an oversized tap, so when you walked up the stairs to go inside you were entering through a big tap. Everything was mock colonial, polished wood and orange-coloured vinyl, and since I was giddy from drinking all the colours blended into one broad brushstroke. Terri's friends — two women and a tall man with a ponytail — were already there. She said their names, we said hello, but they didn't register with me, so I can't describe them now.

We drank sweet alcoholic ciders and when the staff placed hot damper on the bar (which they did from time to time) I attacked it like a whaler that had fortuitously stumbled on an injured seal. (If I don't eat between 6.00 and 6.30 I get cranky.) My bum got sore because the colonial-style bar stools were hard (I have flat buttocks), plus Terri was leaning on me and stroking the front of my neck with her fingers. So I had her body weight to contend with as well. Despite the pressure on my lower back and the acute angle of my head, her fingernails certainly created a very pleasant sensation on my neck. I hadn't worked up enough confidence to touch her, but I was close. I played with her fingers a few times, but I didn't want to seem like a playboy. I wanted her to make the first move. But as I got drunker I got braver and as I got braver I got more demonstrative — tangling my leg in hers, touching her thigh with the back of my hand, that sort of thing. I even trotted out some funny noises — *Haathera*, lip trumpet, skeleton teeth — that seemed to further my cause. I became a funny noise guy in Year 9 and things turned around, so naturally in times of doubt you go to what you know. Anyway, the funny noises seemed to do the trick because Terri's friends kept asking me to do them again and again.

. Every time I sat on the bar stool Terri stood between my legs and pressed her body onto mine. From time to time she made these tiny pulsing movements that were perfectly in time with whatever song was playing on the mobile disco machine. It was incredible. I had this sensation my insides were on the outside and all the people in the wine bar could see my innermost secrets. Three months ago I'd never had a girlfriend, I'd never said 'I love you' to anyone (except relatives), and I'd only flirted indirectly — ie, sexy banter with married people. Now I, Sandy, the boy with too much hair on one side of his head was seconds away from kissing an older woman, and tomorrow I'd be going away with a long-term girlfriend. Then Terri ran her index finger slowly down my long nose. She paused at the bump that is central to my nasal design. 'That's a big bump.' Then she ran her finger back up my nose, curiously stopping at the same spot again. She gazed at the bump more closely, like a trained nurse might, then using her thumb and index finger to feel the cartilage she said, 'It's a bit creepy actually.' There's always something to dent your confidence.

Even though I didn't know where to put my hands I was literally willing hers to move towards my sugar banana. In the past I've managed to make things occur by chanting them under my breath. For example, I worried about Dad when he was late home from work, so I'd lie in bed and chant 'Dad come home Dad come home' and it worked. So I chanted 'Lower, lower'. But nothing happened. Maybe that type of thing works when you're younger. I was also at the stage when another drink would cause the room to spin. The images running through my mind were already coloured in with thick red pencil and my hands were beginning to behave like tropical ivy in humid conditions. I was almost out of control. Something had to give — and it did. Without warning, as if someone had inhabited my body, I lunged forward and kissed Terri on the lips, my mouth completely covering hers like I was transferring an orange from me to her via our lips. I watched myself from the comfort of my own shoulder and couldn't believe I was such a bad kisser. I was so hyped up, so full of sweet alcoholic cider I couldn't stop myself moving my mouth bigger, smaller, wider, thinner. Thankfully, Terri took control. She closed my eyes with her fingers and licked the insides of my ear, exploring crevices only ever touched by a warm flannel or a cotton bud. She stared at me, her sleepy expression filling me with uncontrollable lust. 'You'll turn me on if you put your tongue in my ear, swarthy.' That's when I saw Rhys behind the bar. I looked straight at him, he looked straight at me. I couldn't believe it. Rhys was a bloody barman at Tilly's! He must have seen me kiss Terri! He must have! How could he not have seen me kiss Terri? The heat drained from me like a warm foot on cold lino.

'Rhys.'

'Sandy?'

'Under no circumstances tell Virginia what happened here.'

I was frantic, like a man who'd accidentally killed someone on a country road. I should have acted as if this type of thing happens to me all the time. Maybe he'd be impressed that I was with an older woman? No. He'll tell Virginia. There goes my holiday. That's all I could think about — there goes my holiday. Rhys had to serve someone and I used the break to tell Terri I had to go. I think I said, 'Thanks for having me,' like I'd been at someone's place and I was thanking their mother for letting me watch the wrestling. I wish I could have shown more gratitude because it was one of the most stimulating nights of my life, but I guess I was too spooked to show gratitude. I had to run, pretend nothing happened. I wish I could have pretended the four kilometre walk back to the office to get my car was a cab ride.

By the time I got to my car I was tired and cranky. I still didn't know the exact arrangements for tomorrow. At least I was mobile and when you're mobile you get answers faster. My first thought was to drive past Virginia's. If I saw a light I'd crawl along the flowerbox outside her bedroom, tap on her window and tell her what I'd done. If I nipped the situation in the bud everything would be all right. Virginia would see a positive side of me flirting. What if I seemed obsessive and creepy, crawling along her flowerbox? What if she'd spoken to Rhys? Change of plan. Go to Kath's and ask them what's happening tomorrow. If I went to Kath's I could find out if anyone had talked to Rhys while pretending to find out what the exact arrangements were for tomorrow. It would be cool if I dropped by late too. I was still dressed as a Real Estate agent, but if I untucked my shirt and ruffled up my hair I would appear more bohemian.

I drove past Kath's. Surprisingly, both the Statesman and the Valiant were there. I could hear the stereo blaring away. Were they having a party? I parked several houses away, crept up to the house, up the path and tried to hear what was happening inside. I could hear Nerida's laugh over the music. I listened for the sunny sounds of Virginia but I couldn't tell if she was there or not — shrill is louder than sunny. I didn't know what Rhys sounded like so I couldn't listen for him.

I knocked and waited. Nothing. Banged and waited. Nothing. Banged and yelled. Nothing. There was a mail slit in the centre of the multi-coloured door. When I peered through it I could see the first few metres of the hallway. I thought if I could just get my arm through the slit I could reach over and unlock the door myself. I looked about to see if anyone was watching me, rolled up the left sleeve of my lemon work shirt, squeezed my hand through the slit, pushed my forearm in and worked the angles until I got my elbow in. I started feeling for the lock, like a tree snake hunting for wild budgie eggs. I was almost there too, my fingertips were actually touching the lock's outer casing, but I couldn't get any closer because my upper arm was too big to get through the slit. I just couldn't reach in far enough to get a good enough grip on the lock.

Surrounding the mail slit was a weather shield made from a hard rubber that pointed inwards, a bit like a pair of cupped hands. It allowed letters to be pushed in, but it kept the rain out. It gave way easily when I pushed my hand through, but when I tried to withdraw it again my watch caught on it. I tried to pull my hand out, I tried to yank it out, I tried twisting it out, but no matter what I did the watch kept catching on the rubber. It needed someone on the inside to undo my watch for me. (Lucky it wasn't Monday or I'd have to hold their mail.) When you put your hand into the unknown sometimes you do need assistance to remove it again. Anyway, the Bowie music that was drowning everything out finished, Kath obviously heard the knocking and came to investigate. When she first saw my arm inside the door she screamed because she thought I was a robber, but thankfully I have a very distinctive voice and she recognised me before she hit my arm a second time.

Ross, Nerida, Miranda, Virginia and Danny were all inside. Rhys didn't seem to be there. I actually made myself dizzy looking in as many parts of the house as quickly as possible to check if he was there. The TV was on with the sound down — a naked man was standing on an ornate bedhead doing a weird dance while standing over another man and a woman who were lying in the bed. I looked at Danny, we didn't make full eye contact, we just said 'Eh' while staring at each other's chests. I was relieved when Virginia interrupted the awkwardness and made room for me next to her on the green lounge. I didn't like touching Danny's thigh (he had on corduroy pants and every time our thighs touched there was a sound), but I was in between him and Virginia and that was a win.

Since I was fresh meat all the attention turned to me. I explained I'd been at staff drinks and only came over to find out what the arrangements were. I told them the story of how I tried to open the door. No matter what I said they just kept staring at me, so I just kept on talking. It was awful. Virginia eventually saved me when she said she'd left a message with my father about the arrangements. Danny added, 'Pick you up at 4.30 man.' His voice was light and frail which belied his reputation as morose. I'd never spoken to him before. I'd seen him under the Norfolk pines at the southern end of the beach: catching other guys' spit in his mouth, yelling at tourists, wiping human faeces on people's windscreen wipers. I'd watched him surf — he had a busy hot dog style — but this was the closest I'd been to him and I was struck by how pretty his eyes were. They were beautiful. 'Is that all right?' he said apologetically.

'Yes, of course,' I replied, mesmerised by his sky blue stare.

'In four and a half hours' time,' added Nerida.

'We should go, fruit bat,' said Ross in his cartoon-like way. 'It's a bloody long drive tomorrow.'

Miranda interrupted. 'Another nail, slag?'

I guess that was drug talk.

I was too afraid to ask if anyone had talked to Rhys in the last hour, but until I was sure no one knew about Terri and me I was unable to leave. I really tried to watch everyone closely for some type of sign they knew — exchanged looks, raised eyebrows, talking in code and so on. However, everything changed the moment Kath mentioned (in passing) that Rhys would be home soon. After that I couldn't leave fast enough. It was as if I was a pigeon and someone clapped their hands. I was up and moving. Using only my eyes I frantically asked Virginia if she wanted a lift home with me because I was leaving right now. She was reluctant, and seemed surprised by my sudden need to go, but when I acted hurt (still using my eyes) that swayed it my way. I was pissed off that she asked Danny if it was all right for her to go with me. To his credit he told her he didn't mind. (Using just his eyes.) Nice is a good hiding place. My anxiety was not helped by Virginia's need to say goodbye to everyone individually. She insisted on kissing everybody goodnight and because her kisses take so long it took ten minutes to do everyone properly. I literally had to cut her away from Miranda — they were locked together like two corpses who'd died in frightening circumstances. *(NB She and Danny didn't touch. I immediately thought of something someone had once told me. When two people stop touching it means they've done it. Apart from Virginia Nerida was the only person who touched me. If my theory holds true I'd done it with everyone in the room except Virginia and Nerida. NB I may need to rethink my theory.)*

In the car on the way to Virginia's I initiated all the conversation. It was horrible.

'Why didn't you want to come with me?' I said.

'Danny took me, it's only courtesy I see if he wants to drop me home.'

'Why did he pick you up?'

'He wanted to talk about something.'

'What?'

'None of your business.'

(Silence.)

'Has anyone talked to Rhys tonight?' I asked in a way that suggested I was making idle conversation, hiding the fact I was feeling her out to see if she'd heard from him about me at Tilly's.

'He's at work, babe.'

'Whose car is he in tomorrow?'

'You got a problem with him, babe?'

'No.'

'You're always asking about him.'

My smokescreen had blown away. I was exposed, but not for the reason I should've been exposed. Sure Rhys was the first openly gay person I'd met, but I was not threatened by that. I was frightened by what he knew, but I couldn't tell Virginia that. I thought I may have to act a little gay tomorrow to make sure no one else misunderstood me.

'Was there a party tonight?'

'No.'

'How come Danny was there?'

'I told you why.'

'He always looks depressed.'

'Does he?'

(For some reason the following question popped into my head.)

'Was he good in bed?'

'You're so juvenile sometimes.'

'That's what gives me my charm.' *(She laughed.)*

'He got good with practice.' *(I didn't find that funny, but I laughed.)*

When I got home I crept in without turning on the lights because I didn't want to wake anyone. I imagined I was a French Resistance fighter creeping past enemy soldiers in a field covered with dry leaves, which made it quite fun. With that in mind I reached our thin apricot-coloured hallway without mishap and passed the master bedroom, my father's snoring cancelling out the noisy floorboards near the doorway. Sadly, as I crept by the spare room, two metres from my own bedroom door, disaster struck. Like a phantom from the Dreamtime my Aunty Coral suddenly appeared dressed in a pale pink nightie, her little round turtle eyes blinking as they adjusted to the dim night-light in the hall.

'Clive?'

'No Aunty Coral, it's Sandy.'

'Steak sandwich?'

'No thanks, Aunty Coral.'

'I'll make you a steak sandwich.'

'No thanks, Aunty Coral.'

'Come on ... I'll make you a steak sandwich.'

'Okay.'

I sat at the kitchen table while Aunty Coral prepared the steak sandwich. We didn't talk much. I don't think she was awake — she was in a state of suspended selflessness. Coral wasn't really my aunty. She was a well-meaning family friend who'd lost her husband.

Coral seemed smaller than I remember. Maybe her nightwear created that illusion. It was certainly a big nightie. The back hung down in a straight line from her shoulders like a painter's drop sheet. You got the feeling a puppeteer could have been hiding in there waiting to put on a show. I was also aware of a sadness surrounding her, but that could have been me feeling guilty about not picking her up from the airport, or me feeling guilty about going away, or because she didn't know where anything was and I was making no effort to help.

The steak sandwich tasted good. An expertly made steak sandwich indeed — steak, tomato, lettuce, onions, salt and tomato sauce. The only thing that could have improved it would have been an egg. (I'd have been pushing it if I asked for an egg at 12.55 am.) One shouldn't eat a big meal before bed, but what the heck! I was going to have a restless night anyway, what with all the things on my mind, and to be honest once the salty taste of the tomato sauce was established in my mouth I found that I was quite hungry. It was probably a good thing to have something solid in my stomach to offset the cider. Our family are notoriously bilious people.

(Faithful re-creation of dialogue.)

'It's a bummer you didn't come last weekend Aunty Coral, because I'm going away tomorrow ... for eight days.'

'How was your steak sandwich?'

(I'd forgotten she replaced emotion with food. Aunty Coral found it easier to make a sandwich than to communicate with someone.)

'I'm going away for Christmas this year, Aunty Coral.'

'I don't get to cook for people any more.'

Coral was out of practice with listening. I suppose she had lots of things to talk at, but no one to listen to. She had her dog called Amigo, a little Sydney silky, but he was no great conversationalist. Whenever you were with Aunty Coral you had to remind yourself she was very lonely. When I slept over there I discovered that she even left the windows open at night so the breeze would create some noises around the house. I remember once when I tried to close them she stopped me and said 'The breeze makes it feel like Clive is still pottering around the house.'

Christ, it's 2.40 am.

Saturday 21 December

4.00 am. When the alarm went off it felt as if I'd had 40 seconds' sleep and I had a headache. You imagine how things might be, what you might say on a particular day, but it's never the way you imagine. I wanted to be a marine biologist, but I ended up in Real Estate. I thought there'd be one compare and contrast question in my Year 12 English paper — there were two. I thought I'd feel like a million dollars on the first morning of my holiday, but I felt like a handful of copper coins. I removed my bag from where I'd hidden it at the back of the cupboard. I put on the clothes I'd planned to wear — a long T-shirt with a zipper (it made my chest look stronger and hid my paunch), cotton jeans, desert boots and I packed the journal I'm now writing in, plus three blue pens. Under the influence of sweet apple cider last night I'd obviously packed rather haphazardly because my bag looked like a fat leg with cysts. It didn't look as cosmopolitan as I'd planned and that was disappointing.

Everything around me looked different: my pennants, the trophy for best club man, the surfing pictures I'd put on the wall in case important friends came over. Perhaps everything was different because it was still dark? Perhaps everything felt different because last night was so weird? I certainly felt a little indestructible this morning, like I could swim into the side of a pool and not hurt myself. I say this because when my knee caught the side of the bed it didn't hurt. Normally I have absolutely no tolerance to pain. Despite the vascular headache and the prospect of being constipated for several days (never eat steak after midnight), I felt strong, confident and free. A bit of self-esteem is a great deadener.

I'd forgotten Dad wanders about the house before sunrise. He only sleeps five hours, using the quiet time before dawn to worry about our family. Mum told me not to be frightened if I ever heard noises during the night, it was only Dad crunching on a piece of toast, moving ornaments around or pacing about. After the initial fright I got from running into him in the kitchen passed, I said 'Hi' as if it was the most natural thing in the world for us to be together at 4.15 am. I grabbed a glass of water, partly because I was thirsty, partly because it delayed our inevitable confrontation, partly because I felt better with something in my hands.

'I'll see you in eight days then,' I said. *(Here it comes. Here comes the big stopper. Tell me I can't go away.)* 'See ya then,' I said, giving him another chance to prevent me from going away.

At this point I usually get a discourse about road safety, or what to do if I see a client of his, but on this morning, zero, except a friendly, 'Sure you don't want some breakfast?' Very sneaky. Trying to get to me by using food as a substitute for emotion, eh?

'No thanks. I have to get ready.'

'Right you are then,' he replied — a stock phrase that says nothing but hides a great deal. We were like two friends who were not sure whether to shake hands or embrace. But in the end we did neither, leaving both parties dissatisfied. I left for the bathroom, partly because

I felt awkward, partly because I wanted to say goodbye to it as well. After all, it was like family to me and it might be the last friendly toilet I'd experience for eight days. Then I fetched my surfboard and sleeping bag from under the bed and piled everything in a heap on the front verandah, all the time thinking, What's a great last thing to say to Dad?

Dad was tearing GLAD Wrap off a bowl of leftovers — probably my dinner from last night. He stopped what he was doing, as if I'd returned before he was ready. We stood half a metre apart shuffling our feet like two nervous swimmers. He looked at my forehead, I stared at his chest. Then he reached into the pocket of his gown, took out $100 note, folded it several times, pressed it into my palm and closed my fingers over it. Neither of us knew what to do. The leftovers were still cold and not ready to act as a substitute for genuine emotion yet — hot food is a better substitute for emotion than cold food. I wanted to hug him, my arms were twitching in anticipation of hugging him but nothing happened. I'd hug more people if I didn't feel like I was always going to headbutt them. I never know where to position my head. (My family has a lot of scar tissue around the eyebrows.) I tried to give the moment weight by making eye contact for longer than seemed natural, but when I thought about prolonged eye contact I thought about Virginia. When I thought about Virginia I thought about Terri. When I thought about Terri I thought about Virginia, and when I thought about Virginia I felt guilty. So instead of saying anything meaningful I just lightly touched my father on the shoulder with the palm of my hand, turned away from him and walked down the hallway without looking back. I almost had a big moment with my father that neither of us will ever talk about again.

I could feel my cargo of guilt weighing me down, making it hard for me to glide across the treacherous sandbar at the entrance to our family harbour. I must admit, as I stood outside on the narrow verandah waiting for Danny to pick me up, I was relieved to see the outside light come on because it meant that my father was still thinking about me too. (I think the sensor light was the one in the backyard.)

Two headlights appeared at the southern end of our street, like two outstretched arms feeling their way in the dark. It was Danny's Statesman. You could tell from the frustrated rumble of the engine — his car always sounds like it wants to go faster. Then it struck me — I was actually going away. Shit! I thought about how wonderful steak and onion gravy is when it's reheated, especially on toast covered with a liberal amount of butter. I hoped missing my breakfast wouldn't put me off balance for the rest of the day. The things that go through your head sometimes!

The Statesman stopped defiantly across our driveway and Virginia bounded out like an animal released by the RSPCA. I had to shush her without seeming prudish because it was a conservative neighbourhood. She looked healthy in her cheesecloth top and tiny denim shorts. Danny and I went 'Eh' to each other.

'Do you want me to put this stuff in the boot, babe?'

'Cool.' (*I never say cool.*)

'I'll put your board on top, man,' mumbled Danny.

'Cool.'

'Wow they're sharp rails, man. You only surf the big waves or what?'

I said yes, but I realised Danny's comment was probably ironic, so I quickly added 'Der' to undermine myself just in case he was making fun of me.

I got in the back of the Statesman. It smelt bad. The smell you get when carpet is wet. Virginia got into the front seat. Why didn't she get in the back with me? To compensate she leaned over and kissed me twice. That was better. 'Look at me, Danny,' I said, using just my right eye. 'We're kissing and you're not. Stick that in your pipe, Norfolk boy!' The frustrated rumble of his engine helped me to keep on kissing longer because noise always makes me feel less inhibited. (NB *At the steelworks I made friends and I put that down to loud industrial noise*.) Virginia and I continued kissing as the car pulled away. I even dragged her into the back seat, her elbow landing directly on my sternum, but I doggedly kissed on. I knew how important it was for me to show some affection in front of Danny early on. I think Virginia liked me being assertive too, or was she offended by my possessiveness? (Why does there have to be two sides to a point?) I only broke off our embrace to look back towards my house. We were at the point in the street where my go-cart tipped over and I went face first into the bitumen. We were at the point in the street I was never allowed to go past because it meant I'd be out of eyesight. Suddenly, as if it had been scripted, the outside light on our verandah went off. At least I knew that the sensor light was the one in the backyard.

11.20 pm. Woke up at the Big Banana. The last thing I remember was the Gosford turn-off. Virginia must have been asleep too because she had creases on her face that looked like surgery scars. If I'd put texta slashes across them they'd have looked like stitches. I'd never seen her after she'd woken up. She seemed vulnerable and her mouth clicked because it was obviously dry. I knew her mum's first name, I'd just seen her after she'd woken up — we were two points away from being great friends (according to my list). As usual, Danny was sullen. Obviously he hated me spoiling his plans with Virginia. Obviously I enjoyed that. Stick that in your pipe and smoke it, Norfolk boy. Sometimes cool people are just depressed folk. Danny fitted into that category perfectly.

Five hours! Quick trip. Danny must have driven fast to beat Shaun. I'd have helped with the driving except the Statesman was manual and I drive automatic. (*NB Why do they make cars that go so far over the speed limit? If you get a speeding ticket you should give it to the manufacturer.*) (*NB Good topic for after-dinner discussion.*)

I was hungry and couldn't wait for the others (I bet Ross was driving slowly to ensure his $10 bet was safe), so I had a caramel malted milkshake and a toasted cheese, tomato and ham sandwich while I waited. It's impossible for me to spoil a meal. A family trait — we can never spoil a meal. I also bought three Golden Roughs, one for Danny, Virginia and me, but I ate Danny's before I saw him. I rate the Golden Rough number one when it comes to chocolate. 1: Golden Rough. 2: Chokito. 3: Flake. 4: Picnic. 5: White chocolate.

Shaun, Kath and Miranda arrived ten minutes later. How courageous was Kath to wear a dress made out of hessian bags at the Big Banana? The dress, combined with her bucket handbag, literally drew gasps from the conservative types wandering about looking for something to admire.

First surprise of my holiday. While searching through my bag for lip balm I found a parcel of freshly cut sandwiches. My mother must have packed them last night. She'd also included a packet of shortbread biscuits. That means she must have known where I was hiding my travel bag. I wonder if she knew about the loose parquetry tiles in the rumpus room where I kept the saucy pages I'd torn from Dad's copy of *Valley of the Dolls* and a pair of ladies' silk bloomers I'd found in our laundry? I was quite moved by the sandwiches (ham and lettuce), but it meant there were very few hiding places in a close-knit family. I was glad she hadn't put any tomato on the sandwiches. Tomato would have gone soggy. Tomatoes do not carry emotion as well as ham. *(NB Another post-dinner discussion topic?)*

Ross was ten minutes behind Shaun. I prepared for his arrival (I knew Rhys would be with them) by getting in the back seat of the Statesman and pretending to be asleep. I didn't want to confront Rhys until I felt settled. The best way to deal with a problem is to hide. Where's the best place to hide? Answer: sleep. I kept the shortbreads with me so I had something to nibble on if I got bored waiting for them to notice that I was asleep. It was fun seeing how slowly I could eat a biscuit. It added levity to an otherwise tense situation. I needn't have worried about trying to feign sleep. The inside of the car was so humid I drifted in and out of consciousness naturally. I didn't hear much of what was going on outside the car at all. I didn't even hear Ross arrive.

One of my pet hates on a driving holiday is stopping. My father is the same. Mum literally has to force him to stop if we need to go to the toilet. 'Stick your bum out the window,' he'd say. I'd obviously inherited that gene because when we stopped to watch some ducks cross the road I could have punched someone in the face. When you've been in a car a long time you get this sensation that you're moving quickly and when you stop everything seems painfully slow. We were so close to the shed yet for ten bloody minutes (it seemed like hours) we stopped to watch these stupid ducks cross the

bloody road. *(NB I wonder if ducks have only children? Another post-dinner discussion topic.)*

Miranda joined our car at this point. (While we were watching the ducks Kath and Shaun went ahead to get a key for the shed.) She sat in the back with me. When she wasn't leaning forward to rub Virginia's shoulders she filmed anything that seemed interesting on her video camera. When she pointed it at me I sang a song I'd made up called 'Mr Alley Cat'. (See page 152)

> *Alley cat,*
> *Box head toughie,*
> *You're rather scruffy,*
> *Don't you run away from me.*
> *Alley cat, manners so deplorable,*
> *Still you're adorable.*
> *I love you, oh don't you see.*

I'd be interested to see that back at some stage.

I knew from Kath's map that we must be very close, however the more I wanted to arrive at the shed the longer it seemed to take. Every single second seemed to carry the burden of anticipation. I saw a sign advertising the Woody Head Caravan Park and I wondered if the singles would be allowed to enter the shed, or would they be sent straight on to Woody Head? I hoped so. I didn't want Danny or Miranda to be around at the shed and I certainly didn't want Rhys around. Not until I had a chance to talk with him and that was impossible because I was too busy avoiding him.

'There's the big slag there,' yelled Miranda, pointing to the squat figure of Kath standing on a silver gate. Miranda stuck her head out the window and screamed, 'Slag! Slag!' Kath waved back like an excited feral who'd just received an arts grant, while Shaun stood behind her pretending to have wild sex. Miranda screamed, 'Sluts! Sluts!' and pointed the camera at them. 'Do something funny! Do something funny!' I felt like tapping Miranda on the shoulder and saying, 'They are doing something funny, Miranda.'

Danny manoeuvred his Statesman through the gate (Ross was directly behind), then Shaun and Kath jumped up on the bonnet of his car. The track was bumpy and they were like two tea bags jiggling up and down as they barked out directions and pointed to things of interest. In Danny's car Kath was the point of interest because her hessian dress had stuck to her back and we could see her undies. 'Tell her,' said Virginia.

'No no,' cried Miranda (who was filming the whole thing). 'It's funny.'

I was with Miranda, I thought it was very funny too.

There were small gum trees scattered about the paddock and twenty or so cows grazing in groups of three or four. The ones that lingered on the track barely moved as we drove up close to them. They had a look in their eye that said 'Get stuffed, we live here'. Virginia declared her undying love for cattle by winding down the window and saying as much. 'I love you, cattle.' (How daggy.) Kath pointed left, so Danny veered that way until we reached another fence and another silver gate. It was like a minimum-security prison.

Virginia barely waited for the car to stop moving before she bounded out to open the gate. Instead of getting back in the car after she closed it she ran in front of us going 'Woah' and waving her arms above her head as if she was carrying a large malleable piece of foam. Nerida was doing the same in front of Ross's Valiant, except her imaginary piece of foam was bigger and more malleable. Then, suddenly, there it was — the grey besser brick shed with a flat roof. It was smaller than I imagined it and at first glance you'd have to say it lacked a distinguishing feature. If I had to write the copy for our display window at work I'd stress ambience of location rather than the shed itself, although a small block of red brick units next door did spoil the ambience somewhat. The township of Iluka was creeping closer all the time. As the cars pulled up and everyone piled out, acting like they'd won a grand final, I felt apprehensive. I tried to join in on the communal whooping but two things prevented me. Direct eye contact with Rhys and my first step towards the shed was met with a foot full of bindies.

As Kath opened the door an unsettling rush of hot air poured out. 'The heat from a previous holiday,' quipped Miranda. I reached out for Virginia, hoping we could enter together, but she was already inside. It took quite a while for my eyes to adjust to the darkness, so at first the inside of the shed seemed rather dreamlike and mysterious. However, as I adapted the dream became a large tiled room with a chipboard partition across one-third of it: sink, stove, shelves, a laminex table, a few old lounge chairs, kero lamps and an old double bed. I walked around the partition — two queen-sized beds were set side by side. Shaun and Kath were already lying on one bed rubbing each other and me watching them didn't disturb them at all. Directly behind them were two cubicles — a shower in one and a toilet with a plastic curtain for a door in the other. I could not use a toilet that only had a curtain for a door. My ablutions sound like a large merchant boat entering a foggy harbour and the smells I create easily transcend plastic. I'd have to scout around for more private

amenities or hold on for eight days. At least Virginia and I were separated from the others because our bed was on the other side of the partition — 'in limbo', as Shaun put it. 'Where the couple hoping to gain full pre-established status waits.' Unfortunately, the centre of our mattress had a ravine carved into it.

'We'll need a rope ladder to get out of here,' said Virginia.

Ross smiled at her joke. 'Limbo is not meant to be easy.'

My lips smiled, but what he didn't seem to realise was my eyes were saying 'Prick'.

We unloaded the cars. I kept fake busy, putting my hand on things already being carried by two or more people and grimacing. I'm good at fake busy. I needed to be. Ross had brought every variety of camping equipment known to the human race: bush shower, kayak, mosquito net, fishing gear, first-aid kit, oilskins, underwater camera, snorkelling gear and so on. We resembled a trail of Argentine ants stretching from his Valiant to various parts of the grey shed. My essentials list seemed so self-absorbed compared to his. If we were both bower-birds I'd have seemed lacking in the shiny object department.

My confrontation with Rhys almost occurred when we had to carry Ross's kayak round the back of the shed. He was at one end and I was at the other. The hull more or less reflected what was between us — something lightweight but difficult to manoeuvre.

'Good trip?' I asked.

'Torture.'

Maybe he didn't remember anything?

After getting all the stuff out of the cars Kath told us we were invited to dinner with her mum and dad. I assumed that meant singles and couples. I was beginning to worry that the singles would never leave. On the other hand, I was eager to meet some parents who didn't smother their offspring.

Had the first shower in the shed. The nozzle was loose and the water came out so hard it literally cut my skin. Afterwards the top of my chest was bright red. If you had a long shower you'd need to go to casualty and get stitches. There was also a frog near the cold tap, so I had to have my shower hotter than I would have liked because I was reluctant to fiddle with the cold tap in case the frog jumped on my hand. I didn't like being watched either. No matter where I moved its eyes followed me. I suppose I was doing the same to it.

Owen and Tina have a two-storey blond brick house with interrupted views of canefields and the wide black river that had followed us since Grafton. It was like any house on any suburban street in any provincial city. I'd pictured mudbrick or a log cabin, and I'd imagined Owen as tall with long grey hair tied in a ponytail, brown leathery skin, wearing a poncho with a Mexican motif on it. I'd imagined Tina as strongly built with wild attractive eyes and a spitfire voice. Owen was squat and square with a paunch shaped like a baseball mound, rheumy eyes and he was unfriendly. He gave me the impression he forced himself to be interested in you. Tina was small, frail and blotchy. She looked as if she'd been sick for a long time. Her skin was the colour of tobacco and she seemed to complain about humidity all the time. When she showed Virginia and I some of her leatherwork in a small airless studio at the side of the house, I said to Virginia, 'This is not the work of a happy person.'

We had ratatouille and baked pumpkin for dinner. There wasn't enough, so I offered to take the dirty dishes to the kitchen just so I could lick the plates and look for any scraps that were lying around. I'd say the first meal was below expectations. Quality and taste were fine, quantity well below what is necessary to sustain a middle-class life.

During dinner everyone talked adult about Owen's plans for the farm and his idea to create an 'executive chill-out pad'. He wanted to construct teepees then advertise in Sydney for stressed-out executives to come and relax in them. I imagined Mr Wunderlich sitting in a teepee, or Mr Fewings, and somehow the concept didn't gel for me.

Ross was also made to honour his bet for being wrong about how long the drive up here would take. We tried not to laugh at him, but the expression on his face was priceless and Virginia and Kath couldn't contain themselves. Virginia was the worst. During one fit of laughter she spat a lump of pre-chewed food the size of a golf ball onto Kath's lap. I haven't laughed so much in ages.

During dinner I had no opinions about anything. Talking and chewing are traditionally two separate events in our family. Surprisingly, when Owen asked me a question (while I was chewing) and I replied, 'Can't talk and eat at the same time', everyone laughed at me. I don't think they realised I meant it. But it did open my eyes to the fact I could probably continue my normal patterns of behaviour up here providing I made fun of them.

After dinner we sat outside and drank wine. Everyone talked softly and looked quite handsome by the light of the fire. Couples snuggled, touched and pecked — I bet the singles felt out of it — although Miranda did her best to muscle in on the action by laying her head in Virginia's lap and encouraging the latter to stroke her hair. I also tried to keep myself between Rhys and Virginia without being too obvious. The only time I looked suspicious was when he was about to sit down next to her once and I rushed over and beat him to the seat. I tried to be as friendly as possible towards Rhys, adding a 'darling' to the end of my sentences whenever I could: 'Pass the wine, darling.' If we appeared similar he might be less inclined to say anything about Terri. It's easier to love someone that reminds you of yourself. Adding a 'darling' to the end of sentences really made stock phrases sound more natural too. I might try and make it a habit.

It was difficult for me to blossom with Danny hanging around. He'd been to the hobby farm before, he'd helped Owen lay the foundations for the shed and this familiarity made him appear like the boyfriend, not me. At least Owen knew his name. Whenever he talked with me he had to pause a second and think of my name first. That's why when Owen mentioned he was building a boatshed I jumped at the chance to help out. It meant next time I came here for a visit I'd have a solid foundation to build on.

Afterwards, as we strolled back to the shed, the couples paired off and talked confidentially while the singles trailed behind. I mentioned to Virginia how Owen and Tina were not what I expected. I also noticed there appeared to be tension between Kath and her father.

(Faithful re-creation of dialogue between Virginia and myself.)

'Since her folks moved here there's been super tension in the family. The idea of coming here was a total obsession with Owen. When Kath was younger he'd leave her and Lyn with his brother and drive Tina all over the east coast looking for the perfect piece of land — warm climate, close to a river, close to the sea, 40 acres on a gentle slope. When he found this place he sold his car business and put the family house on the market. But Tina didn't want to move. She had her own friends, she co-owned this florist's shop. Owen dragged her here and now everyone resents him for it.'

'Perhaps that's why Kath had so much freedom ... her parents were away all the time?'

'Very observant, babe.'

This walk was my favourite bit of the trip so far. It felt like we were a married couple returning from a dinner party.

10.35 pm. The singles departed. Hooray! Shaun made a plan to meet for a surf tomorrow. Danny said yes without seeming wild about the idea. Bummer! Shaun asked me if I wanted to go for a surf too. I felt inclined to hang at the shed and act married, but I knew that would sound naff so I said yes.

INTERESTING DEVELOPMENT! On seeing a group discussion that didn't include her Kath literally sprinted over and took command. 'The first thing we need to do tomorrow is buy groceries.' Kath only likes to work with her own ideas.

11.15 pm. I wear whatever I've worn during the day to bed, so on this particular night, as I slipped in between the sheets, I wore a long T-shirt with a zipper and no pants. (It was too hot for sleeping bags.) I usually wear underpants too, but I thought I might appear repressed, so I took them off and hid them under my pillow. I love fresh cotton sheets. I like to lie in one spot then measure how far my body warmth radiates out on the sheet. Two centimetres from the body was my record. (*NB When measuring human warmth mark a spot where your partner's body is and then measure how far out the sheets are still warm.*)

Virginia was the last person up. Was she stalling? Was she teasing me? What would she wear to bed? A negligee? French underwear? She lowered herself onto the bed and stretched out beside me. How good was this, knowing I didn't have to leave in half an hour, knowing if I moved two centimetres to my right I'd touch her, four centimetres and we'd be hugging, five centimetres and we'd be doing it. She leaned over and pecked my lips, the pleasant smell of Colgate filled my mouth, then she rolled back and faced the other way. I rolled towards her and stroked her back.

'Virginia sleeps nude, eh?'

'That's nice, babe,' she whispered, referring to the way my hand was lazily floating up and down her spine — my fingernails acting like little dancing pumps on her vertebrae. It's amazing how lust can give you lightness of touch and the stamina to keep stroking. Everyone said good night to each other.

'Good night, Kath.'

'Night, Gin.'

'Night, Sandy.'

'Night, Kath.'

'Night, Shaun.'

'Night, Sandy'

'Night, Ginny.'

'Night, Shaun.'

'Night, Nerida.'

'Night, Sandy.'

'Night, Ginny'

'Night, Neri.'

'Night, Ross.'

The longer it went on the funnier it became. (My second

favourite moment so far.) All the time this was happening I kept trawling Virginia's spine with my fingers, fishing for some return affection. My biceps were aching because there was no support under the arm, but she had said she liked what I was doing so I kept going.

The human body is made up of 90 per cent praise. It's amazing how long we can keep going on so little. After a while I noticed her breathing was heavier — she was either aroused or asleep, but since she was facing away from me I wasn't sure which. So I just kept stroking/listening/waiting until I had more evidence to go on. Perhaps if I pictured what I'd like to happen she'd respond accordingly. Nothing. I repeated to myself, 'Roll over and touch me' about twenty times. I suppose it was just good to be in a double bed with her. Tomorrow morning I'd wake up next to her whereas Danny was at a caravan park, probably in a van that sloped down at one end and he'd wake up with a bright red face. I felt how wonderfully warm the sheet was close to her body. Three centimetres of pure human warmth. I suppose if I was going to make a move it had to be now. I rolled closer to her and gently whispered, 'I love you.' Even though it was barely audible I gave it everything I had. Nothing. So I slunk back onto my side of the ravine and sifted through some stock anxieties, like I always do before going to sleep.

I thought about cooking, the eisteddfod, the toilets, my parents. Then I focused on the recurring dream I've had since I was nine where I'm the captain of a merchant vessel that has stopped for repairs in a Norwegian fiord. Like two familiar arms hugging me at an airport, my dream arrived right on cue. Instantly it took away the discomfort of the strange pillow, the unfamiliar silence of a country area and it put me quietly down to sleep. I was almost out to it when I suddenly heard a repetitive gasping sound, like someone being smothered by a pillow, and an anxious voice saying 'I want to kiss your body all over. I want to kiss your body all over.' Someone was having sex on the other side of the partition and I could hear everything. It was the first time I'd ever heard the sound of other people's sex and I was compelled to listen because other people's privacy is always compelling, but if I could hear them they could hear me. Then Virginia stirred. 'Don't stop rubbing babe, it's soooo nice.'

Sometimes it's hard to show affection.

Lights out was at 11.55 pm.

Sunday 22 December

Had a weird dream last night. I was walking along on a shell-encrusted beach, I went up to a hyena holding a thermos of coffee and asked him, 'Which way is it to the mountain?' He mouthed the words 'Over there.' It was at that point the smell of toast and the sound of cutlery tore my eyes open. Lucky my eyes weren't stuck together with sticky residue, or I would've literally ripped my eyelashes out. (I'm prone to conjunctivitis when I get run down.)

I was starving, but the first thing I saw was the angular figure of Ross and it almost turned me off food for life. He had on shorts and no shirt, his shoulder blades looked like two crooked flagstones on a thin garden path and because his pants were green his legs looked like two cane sticks holding up an indoor fern. He had lots of pimples on his back too. I bet if I joined them up with a pen it would make a giant set of genitals. I watched him through half-closed eyes. I wanted him to think I was asleep, then at the right moment I'd open my eyes, make some exasperated sounds and he'd think he'd woken me up and offer me some of what he was making to compensate for waking me up.

Run-down of Ross's breakfast ritual:

While his toast was in the toaster Ross stood by with butter already sitting on the blade of his knife. He was like an overzealous manager waiting for his rock star client to come offstage. Before that he'd cut up a mango, slicing off the sides with the skill of a surgeon, cutting them into cubes and catching the excess juice in a glass before it ran off towards the sink. Then he covered the glass with plastic and put it in the fridge. How anal is that? He shits me! He also peeled and sliced a banana that had his name written in texta on the skin. When his toast finally popped up he buttered each slice in a blur, spun the teapot three times, poured two teas with a jerking movement, as if it were a technique he'd picked up from a nanna in Condobolin, then he put a saucer over one cup, took a plate with toast and a few slices of mango and banana on it and a cup of tea into Nerida. (I assume it was Nerida.) I opened my eyes as wide as possible ready for his return.

'Sorry, did I wake you up?'

'Yes.'

'Sorry.'

My plan worked perfectly. I had to make him feel guilty enough to make me breakfast otherwise who else would feed me? He stared at me, then at the teapot, at me, then at the teapot. I think he was asking me if I wanted tea? I don't drink tea but it felt as if lantana was growing on my tongue, so I nodded yes. Then I hauled myself up the vertical sides of the mattress. Virginia was still asleep down in the valley. Her mouth was open and there was a damp patch beside her face on the pillow. Should have brought a floral pillowslip like me, darling.

As I unfolded next to my bed, rather like a piece of plastic that had been scrunched up in the bin, Ross glanced at me, as men do when another man is semi-naked in front of them. A full look at the genitals is rude, but little bird-like glances towards the crotch area is commonplace and quite acceptable. If you seem inhibited in front of another man when you're naked it looks as if you've got something to hide. I had something to hide, but to give him the impression I didn't have anything to hide I acted as if I didn't have anything to hide. Ross used his eyes to ask how I had tea? I'd never made tea before, so I used my eyes to say 'I don't care.' He asked me another question with his eyes, but what he was asking was unclear. It was not easy for Ross to convey meaning using just his eyes. They're small and over a distance of three metres they're about as expressive as two small pebbles. I got a mug of sweet milky tea, so I guess we must have been talking about how much milk and sugar do I have in my tea? He then said (with his eyes plus head movements) 'Outside.' Since he'd made me the tea I felt obliged to do what he asked. He'd transferred the guilt back to me. Bummer.

We both looked over the canefields and the black river. The vista was less romantic than when we first arrived yesterday, or perhaps it appeared that way because I was standing next to Ross. He certainly picked up on different things from me. For instance, he said to me, 'Owen's put that bloody cabbage tree palm too close to the fence.' Whereas I said, a little while later, looking in the same direction, 'See, near the cabbage tree, there's a hawk hovering in a thermal.' Neither of us took any notice of each other's observations. There was also a lot of silences. After one particularly long one I felt the need to say something, so I asked, 'Are you going to the beach with us then?'

'I'm helping Owen with the boatshed.' (*I wanted to be in on that too.*)

'Owen told me what he had planned. I tell ya, he's got no bloody idea, so I'm helping him get started.' Ross's breath would discolour a white shirt. It was better if I bobbed and weaved to avoid inhaling the stuff, but doing that made me seem odd. How does Nerida put up with it?

'Do you think he'll mind you telling him he's not doing it right?'

'He wants it done correctly, doesn't he?'

Not wanting to engage in more conversation and risk swallowing any more breath I didn't ask any further questions. We both drank our milky teas and from the corner of my good eye I watched him eat the toast he'd failed to offer me. He chewed every mouthful 30 times. I chew four times then swallow. My stomach doesn't let food stay in my mouth that long. Why should a mouth chew all the taste out of food before a stomach gets it? If we stop chewing our food maybe future generations will develop tastebuds in their stomachs.

Everybody had something different for breakfast. Virginia had two crumpets with honey. As she chewed she went 'Mm mm'. Towards the end of the second crumpet it got on my nerves. Nerida had Coco Pops. Shaun just wrapped a sheet round himself for his breakfast and Kath picked up other people's mess and made exasperated sounds. One thing that we did do all together was bitch about Ross. When a person leaves a room in a share house they're obviously considered fair game. I was shocked by the ferocity of their comments, though. When I asked them if they always talked about each other like this Virginia said it was 'constructive backstabbing'.

'Do you talk about me like this when I'm not here?' I said.

'We use the word dickhead a lot more,' Kath replied.

'Only joking, babe.'

'Had you going though, didn't we?' said Shaun.

List of survival tips for a share house:

1 Always be the second last person to go to bed so no one can bitch about you.

2 Be the second person to get up, so no one can bitch about you.

3 Never wear percussive clothing. That way no one can hear you coming so there's a better chance you'll catch them bitching about you.

4 Align yourself with any couples so you are in the majority on most issues.

Kath was adamant we should get groceries before going to the beach. I didn't mind doing shopping, discussing the different brands with our respective partners, talking to people in the checkout line about the weather and so on. Perhaps we could look at Real Estate prices too, applaud houses we thought were well renovated, boo the bad renovations. However, Shaun wanted to go to the beach, Nerida wanted to see Miranda and Rhys and Virginia needed to see Danny, so Kath was outvoted. (Kath wasn't happy.)

I asked Virginia why she had to see Danny so desperately. There was a pause, like everyone knew something I didn't.

'He's had a few bad times lately.' I was getting sick of that line. I nearly said 'Like breaking up with you', but I stopped myself and got sulky instead. I knew I was the boyfriend and if necessary I could spoil everyone's holiday by being sulky if I wanted to, so I didn't feel bad about playing the little black moose. However, as I was moping it suddenly occurred to me I could probably use the toilet at the caravan park if I went with the others to the beach. So I changed from being a shopping supporter to a beach supporter.

Shaun, Virginia, Nerida and I took off at 9.30. Kath had the shits and stayed behind. I might monitor Kath and see how many times we do something she wants to do and what her reaction is when we don't do what she wants. I might make it a competition. She was down 1–0.

The caravan park was about a kilometre outside Iluka and a kilometre from the hobby farm, but it seemed closer because Shaun drove at 110k all the way. He liked to get close to danger, scrap it, then get his daddy to fix it. Daddy was high in BHP and could afford to fix things.

I was led to believe the caravan park was run down, however, on viewing it I thought it was quite nice — pool, games room, spa, manicured lawns, kids running around in clumps like excited clouds of dust, a resident character called Eel Man (he looked like Curly from the Three Stooges) who caught eels and hung them in a sack outside his van. Miranda and Rhys shared a van located close to the manager's office. Danny had one by himself near the entrance. His car was there, but he wasn't. So while Nerida and Shaun visited Rhys and Miranda, and Virginia looked for Danny, I took the opportunity to go to the toilet.

There were plenty of people in the amenities block and it smelt like disinfectant, but the combination of pre-established odour and noise meant I didn't feel inhibited at all. I entered that amenities block like I was the captain of a tennis team with eight high-class candidates to choose a partner from. In an amenities block the last

Rhys and Miranda's van

cubicle is always the most popular because it's the furthest away from the entrance and people tend to feel more isolated there. The first cubicle is popular because when you're in a hurry you grab the nearest thing to you. The second last cubicle is the forgotten one. In a footrace we remember who came first, second, third, fourth and usually last, but we never take much notice of the second last runner. That's why I made friends with the second last cubicle — it was under less scrutiny than the others. When I say I made friends it wasn't the sort of friend I'd write to after my holiday was over. We weren't going to exchange addresses or anything. But when I sat down on its black plastic seat, my weight slightly forward so I wouldn't get a red ring around my bottom, it was the first time in 24 hours I was truly myself. I just had to work out a way to get down here without the others knowing why I was coming. It was like coordinating an affair.

As I meandered back towards the vans (after a blissful twenty minutes with my new friend), accompanied by the hum of washing machines, the percussive sound of thongs and the ping pong of a table tennis ball being hit by two middle-aged men with tan paunches, I saw Virginia and Danny. They weren't touching each other, but they were very close. You could probably just fit a vertical piece of devon in between them. That gap certainly left a lot of room for speculation. Danny looked sullen, like a child who'd had his ball stolen by older kids. Virginia was generating enough sunniness to create life on a hostile planet. I was animated and friendly because I was nervous. Is this what the end of a relationship feels like? I wanted to be nasty towards Danny, even sarcastic, but my nastiness was simply transformed into moroseness covered by this nervy friendliness. 'What's wrong, babe?' Virginia asked me, as if there was nothing odd about this picture. However, before I could even answer the question Shaun appeared from nowhere, as if he'd been hiding under loose soil nearby and yelled, 'Let's go before the onshore hits, man. Come on.' I turned to Nerida, who was looking on at the time.

'What is it with those two?' (Meaning Virginia and Danny.)

Then Nerida said the weirdest thing: 'She collects people.'

Virginia and I sat in the back of Shaun's Datsun 120Y. Danny was in the front passenger seat (Nerida stayed with Rhys and Miranda) and while he sat there, slumped forward like a puppet on its' way to the next poorly attended supermarket show, Virginia massaged his shoulders. Everyone who sat in a passenger seat got a bloody shoulder rub. I'd try and sit there on the way back and see if I got one. I actually started rubbing Shaun's shoulders, not so much to relax Shaun but to highlight the fact that Virginia was touching Danny and not me. I don't know what Shaun made of it, but he didn't tell me to stop rubbing.

Angourie's a legendary north coast break with a reputation for fierce locals, steep take-offs and great right-handers. As you stroll down to the sand there's a sense you're in paradise — lots of trees, deep mysterious blue pools of water, handsome, fit surfers and beautiful women in crochet bikinis. It was not unlike the scene I visualised when I peered through my fringe.

The waves at Angourie today were four foot and glassy. I knew I'd find the take-offs steep, but I could always say, to anyone who was interested, 'Eh, I've surfed Angourie, man.' The three of us paddled out together like friends — joking, chatting and teasing. The spirit of Angourie had obviously entered my body because I glided effortlessly over the clear water like it was the most natural thing in the world. Normally I find paddling difficult. Not only do I feel unbalanced lying on a board because of my paunch, I find paddling exhausting and by the time I get out the back I'm often too pooped to surf much. Today I was keeping up with the others. (Although I was the only one of us told to fuck off by angry local guys. Some people attract anger — I guess I'm one of those.)

Shaun was on a 6 foot 8 board with fliers. Danny had a shorter board with a busy design he'd obviously done himself. I still had the board I got for Christmas four years ago with the exceptionally hard rails and the red distress signal slashed down the middle. Shaun was quite a good surfer. He did all the right manoeuvres without being inspired at any of them. Danny, on the other hand, dropped in under a lip for a tiny tube ride like it was second nature to him. He was excellent. At least my buddies looked the goods. My plan was to catch an unrideable wave and fall off. That way no one could tell if I was shithouse or not. I was from the Brainiac school of surfing. Brainiac being a ginger-haired Norfolk boy who was so lazy he didn't bother catching waves any more. He simply paddled out and let them break on top of him. If you were sitting behind the wave you'd see the tip of his board and bits of his face break through the back of the swell before he was sucked back down inside the wave again. At first you'd think, What an idiot, but when you saw him repeat the procedure ten times you realised he was unique, if a little foolhardy. No one was sure if Brainiac could really surf, but his reputation stayed intact. There's always a niche for a maddie.

I could see Virginia sitting on the sand in a lime crocheted bikini. She had her head tilted back, like a plant anxious to catch every ray of sun possible. She was staring at me or Danny, it could have been either of us because we were sitting so close together. At one point I paddled away from him to see if Virginia's eyeline followed me, but over that distance (100 metres) it was hard to tell if she followed me, stayed on Danny, or if she was observing a third person.

After fifteen minutes I was the only person not a member of the I've-caught-a-wave club. Therefore I had mixed feelings when a local yelled 'Outside' and everyone started paddling out to meet a brace of liquid green Matterhorns coming our way. It was time for me to do something special, but I was petrified of big waves. As I mentioned I don't like risks, but taking them was one way of creating a niche in a complex social scene. Risk-takers are worshipped.

Cowards are teased. So I paddled out towards the sets, veering right to get on the inside of the other surfers and give off the impression I knew what I was doing. At every surfing break there's a crusty old acid casualty who sits further inside than anyone else, and sure enough at Angourie an old hippie on a malibu was way inside me. I thought, Christ! Now I'll have to wait for this prick to get a wave before I can take off. Fortunately, he was slightly deranged because he took off on the first set and went left straight onto the rocks. When he paddled back out he did exactly the same thing again. I guess every beach has its own version of Brainiac.

The sets were much bigger than I expected. I let the first one go, the second and the third as well, but I guess anxiety forced me to paddle for the fourth one. I didn't want to catch it, but it was my only hope of making an impression, or at least providing a comparison. As the momentum of the wave picked me up and thrust me forwards, the spirit of Angourie must have re-entered my body because I felt strangely confident. This spirit was obviously worried about me, it

didn't want a dud surfer to sully its almost perfect waves, so it was helping me out. I looked down the face and as much as I wanted to use the conditions on offer, I resisted the spirit's call for me to stand up. As tempting as it was to succeed, that was not my goal. My goal was to fail, thus keeping my reputation as a guy who'll take off on anything intact. So I waited that little bit too long, when the wall was at its steepest and people would think, He's insane he can't possibly make that. Much to my surprise, however, I stood up and instead of nosediving like I always did, and indeed as I'd planned to do, I made the late take-off. I started across the wave, riding high up on the lip at a frightening speed. I felt like a million dollars. Look at me! I'm surfing Angourie! The very moment I allowed myself the luxury of positive thought I started thinking negative ones. (Family trait.) 'I'm going too fast, I'm too high on the wave', and sure enough the nose of my board dug into the wall and next thing I knew I was airborne, my board spiralling high into the air, trying to escape from me and attach itself to a better surfer. I could now happily paddle back to shore knowing I'd created a lasting impression and no one knew if I could surf or not because I hadn't been on the wave long enough for anyone to find out. I almost let the spirit of a great surfing spot force me to rise to the occasion, but I controlled it with ingrained negativity. Virginia did put some doubt in my mind when she said, 'You should stand up straighter, babe. You're very hunched over when you surf, like you're frightened or something.' At least that solved the question of who she was looking at.

Played cards after dinner. Every time I got a good hand I got the giggles. In other words, every time I looked like winning I became anxious. Shaun said I'm afraid of winning. I think he's right. I also tried out one of my topics for conversation: Why do they build cars that go over the speed limit? Ross said so if you get into trouble you've got the power to get out of trouble. End of discussion.

Thought about Jatz with cheese, cordial, then a salad sandwich. I think cucumber is the secret ingredient on a salad sandwich. You can smell it in advance. When I think about food it's a sure sign I'm relaxed. I fell asleep at 11.30.

Monday 23 December

I'd imagined the river's edge to be a magical place, ripe for contemplation, romance and good for whatever ails ya. At the Greens' hobby farm the shoreline (where the boatshed was being built) was a combination of twisted trees and black mud. If you stepped in the wrong place you sunk to your knees in smelly ooze and it took all your power to pull your legs back out again. There were also swarms of mosquitoes. It was as if the river and the mosquitoes were working in tandem. The mud trapped you, the mosquitoes drained your blood and if you lent on the tea-trees apparently you got ticks as well. On a practical level, it was fun laying the foundations for the boatshed because I got to use all the different tools required to spread cement. I've never been exposed to many tools in my life. My father had only a shovel, a mattock and a hammer. My own tools (Phillips head screwdriver and a pair of pliers) all fitted into a yellow pencil case, so as we spread the cement being poured by a squat man from his mini cement machine I felt like a tradesman with rough hands and tobacco on my breath. All the couples pitched in too, like Quakers putting up a barn in the movie *Witness*. It was interesting to watch Ross and Owen together because they had differences, but since it was Owen's dream Ross had to back off. More than once Ross shuffled over to Nerida mumbling, 'He doesn't know what he's doing.'

I started off shovelling, but I found that too hard. Then I trowelled, but Owen said I was too eager to move on to the next bit. I was best at going up to the house and bringing back tea and biscuits for the workers. Since I was a good listener, Tina gave me extra things to eat. Not only does listening create opportunities to talk about yourself, it comes in handy when you're after a snack as well. (*NB It was not yet 11.00 am and Tina was drinking chilled claret. She put ice cubes in the claret and she used a chilled glass as well.*)

On my second sortie up to the house for refreshments Kath came along too. It was weird. On the way up we didn't say a word. It was obvious neither of us was comfortable with each other. On the way back I was carrying a tray of biscuits, Kath had some beers and I was playing 'Rock Around the Clock' on the lip trumpet, trying to make out I was more relaxed than I really was when Kath said, 'You're funny.'

Thinking she was being sardonic I quickly said, 'Funny in the head?' trying to diffuse her sarcasm with self-deprecation.

'No, funny funny.'

'I didn't think you liked me?'

'I didn't think you liked me?' Then we both shut up.

2.00 pm. The concrete for the boatshed was poured and the seven steel columns set around the perimeter of the slab made the partly built boatshed look like a poor Stonehenge. I was curious to know what the end product would look like. Owen let us put our initials in the cement. I was now on an even playing field with Danny because he had his initials in the floor of the shed.

4.00 pm. Went to a place near Woodburn (south of Ballina) to look at koalas in the wild. (Virginia, Miranda and me.) The squat cement contractor told us, 'Koalas are literally falling out of the fuckin' trees up there, mate.' The image of koalas falling out of trees certainly captured my imagination and I'm happy to say I was the prime mover in getting a party to go there. I'd have liked more than just Miranda, Virginia and me to go, but I'd suggested something and two people responded. My mother always said I was a natural leader.

None of us had access to a car so we were forced to hitchhike. In normal circumstances that would be an obstacle (the danger aspect and all that), but it was my idea and I was more motivated than usual, therefore I did everything I could to make hitchhiking seem romantic. (There's the Real Estate training coming out.) Surprisingly, we only waited ten minutes before being picked up by an off-duty coach captain in his empty tour bus. He dropped us right where we needed to go plus he let us watch twenty minutes of *Ferris Bueller's Day Off* on his in-house video.

The squat contractor was right, there were heaps of koalas up in the trees. So many in fact I was constantly gazing up into the canopy, not watching where I was going, and I walked straight into a picnic bench. The bloody thing caught me across the shin. Virginia was very comforting, though. The benefits from a minor accident can sometimes outweigh the trauma of the injury. People are drawn closer in times of suffering. The other lesson to be learnt was when you're staring upwards you're occasionally going to trip over.

Not so lucky hitching home. We waited two hours for a lift and it was only frustration that forced us into a car driven by a drunk man wearing a top hat and smoking a cigar. For the first five kilometres no one said a thing because the driver's strange apparel and unsettling manner were frightening and we thought we were all going to die. But as it turned out, the man's wife had just given birth to their first child and he was simply euphoric. Thankfully he was a drunk driver who drove slower rather than faster.

6.45 pm. While the others read their books and drank beer at the back of the shed I sought out Nerida and asked her what she'd meant when she said 'Virginia collects people.' I admit my motive was twofold. I did want to know what she meant, but I really liked talking with Nerida. When we talked about a third person, ie Virginia, it didn't appear like flirting. It was flirting, at least on my part.

(Rough re-creation of some actual dialogue.)

'It's the price she pays for being so likeable, Sandy.' *(I liked it when she called me Sandy.)* 'She collects all sorts, but she's too nice to throw anyone away.'

(I think she may have been referring to me.)

The books the others were reading:

Kath was reading *Perfume* by Patrick Suskind.

Virginia was reading the screenplay to *Chinatown*.

Nerida was reading *Emma* by Jane Austen.

Shaun was reading a Boys Town pamphlet about a house they were raffling in the Gold Coast hinterland.

Ross was reading a book called *Strange Planes*.

I stared at *Calypso Cricket* by Roland Fishman, but I didn't read it.

8.00 pm. Lebanese for dinner. I liked it, but I had trouble rolling up the bread to keep my filling inside the roll. I'm not good with my hands. It reminded me of making cane baskets at school. Very fiddly plus you've got to ask yourself is the end product worth the effort. I was not the only person to overfill and lose control of their roll. Shaun overfilled his roll. Ross too, but he held it so he didn't lose any. He tucked his hand under its bottom, like he was holding a baby. Even Rhys overfilled and got an oily stain on his orange blouse. I thought he'd be angry, but he just smeared it wider and said, 'Look everyone, I've got a new brooch.' Danny wasn't there (no one knew where he was), so I'm not sure what he would have done, but he looks like an overfiller to me.

After dinner we played cards (five hundred) and talked about the eisteddfod. Rhys plans to do an impersonation of an international figure. Ross is playing 'In an English Country Garden' on the bottles. Shaun is writing a poem. Nerida is giving a sex lesson. Kath is creating a fire sculpture and Virginia and Miranda were doing something surreal together. I said I'd sing a song called 'Mr Alley Cat'. Miranda said, 'Not the song you sang in the car?'

'Why?'

'Oh nothing.'

That undermined my confidence. Thankfully Virginia distracted me by saying the magic word 'Danny'. 'Danny won't be doing anything in the eisteddfod,' is exactly what she said.

'Why not?' said Nerida.

Rough re-creation of actual dialogue:

'Not his bag.' (Virginia)

'What's wrong with him anyway?' (Shaun)

'What do you mean?' (Virginia)

'He hardly said a word today.' (Shaun)

'He's shy.' (Virginia)

'He looks super down.' (Kath)

'He's all right.' (Virginia)

'He's cute.' (Nerida)

'Settle.' (Ross)

'He is cute.' (Rhys)

'Big?' (Nerida)

'Settle.' (Ross)

'You're obsessed, babe.' (Kath)

'Big enough.' (Virginia)

'Long?' (Nerida)

'Wide.' (Virginia)

'Wide is better than long.' (Rhys)

'Are we playing cards or what?' (Ross)

'Bit threatened, needle dick?' (Miranda)

'I just want to play cards.' (Ross)

'Needle dick.' (Miranda)

The conversation drifted off Danny and on to penises. It was interesting to listen to women chat about penises. I'd heard boys talk about them before, but never women. It seems that wide is better than long. (Good for me.)

This led on to a conversation about the first time we had sex. Kath said she was fifteen. Virginia was only fifteen too and her first partner was actually Danny. It didn't happen until they were six months into their relationship because on their second date Danny unzipped his fly and put her hand on it. 'It was the first time I'd ever felt one and it frightened me and it took six months to get over it.' Despite the trauma of hearing about Virginia with another man, it was funny. If I was Danny I wonder if I would enjoy my private actions being aired in public like this? *(NB Must remember to hide my journal in a different place each night.)*

Nerida's first partner was Ross. I got the feeling she wanted to say something about him, but his eyes were rolling around in their sockets like two small marbles in a glass jar, so she remained mute. Rhys's first time was with a woman and afterwards he cried. Not because it was a woman, but because 'I knew something was not quite right for me'. Miranda's first time was with an apprentice pastry chef and 'they used lots of margarine'. Shaun's first sexual partner was a billet's sister in Griffith NSW. He was fourteen and she was sixteen. He's so bloody up himself, I'm surprised he didn't take off his shirt and twitch his muscles. Ross didn't tell us about his first time, but he did say he'd been married to a Greek woman called Athena. Wow! I've got to get in earlier with stories, when you go last there's so much pressure on your anecdote. I knew I'd sound more interesting if I told a lie, so I said my first time was on a holiday in Fiji and I was only fifteen. It sounded exotic and it was impossible to confirm. I even acted coy to make myself appear vulnerable and therefore more likeable. If it was easy for me to lie about my first time it was easy for the others to exaggerate too.

9.30 pm. Miranda and I washed up. I had this romantic notion about washing up — maybe because it was something my mother and father always did together. My mother washed, my father dried. That was until we got a dishwasher. My father couldn't help after we got the dishwasher because his knees were gone and it was too hard for him to bend down and stack. They got the appliance to make life easier, but it ended up being more work for Mum and humiliating for Dad.

(Faithful re-creation of a traumatic conversation between Miranda and I.)

'How are you and Ginny getting on?' (*Why was she asking me that?*)

'Fine.'

'Sure?'

'Yes.' (*Maybe she knew something about Danny and Virginia?*)

'Do you love her?'

(Why was she asking me that? Perhaps she was interested in Virginia too? Why else would she ask me such a question? I'm such an idiot. Idiot! Idiot! The touching, the rubbing, the head in the lap, the frayed denim shorts, the black singlet. She hadn't specified the gender of the apprentice pastry chef. She was in love with Virginia. Shit! Everyone loves Virginia. I was going out with an Everywoman.)

'Yes.'

'Sure?'

'Yes.'

'If you ever do anything to hurt her ...' *(A bolt of anxiety suddenly shot through my body.)* 'Don't pretend you don't know what I'm talking about.'

'What?'

'She's a beautiful person.'

'Yes.'

'Rhys told me about you.'

(Instead of washing dishes I was smearing them with cold sweat. I tried to batten down as many hatches as I could before they all filled with anxiety and I sunk with all hands on deck.)

'Nothing happened.'

'That's not what he told me, mate.'

'Has he told her?'

'No, but I will.' *(She hit me with a wet tea-towel and it caught me right across the face. I knew I deserved that but it stung and I instantly wanted to go home.)*

'Understand?'

'Yes.'

(I felt like an enemy spy on the verge of having his cover blown. If I could just find a familiar pattern to hide in for a while.)

10.20 pm. Ross drove Miranda and Rhys back to the caravan park. Virginia and Nerida went along to keep him company. As everyone was leaving Miranda really stared at me. I can't stand it when people don't like me. Please like me, Miranda. Please like me. Is this the end?

Kath, Shaun and I sat around the table, ate raisin toast and listened to David Bowie. The music was raucous and the lyrics didn't make sense, but I was glad to have some discord to hide behind. I wasn't comfortable being with just Kath or Shaun. It was bearable when they talked about Danny — Shaun thought he was a psycho, Kath thought it was weird he was even up here. (I was relieved to hear that.) But when they started kissing in front of me it was unsettling. It's odd sitting a metre away from two people kissing passionately. It was like sitting on a crowded beach and the couple next to you are having sex under a beach towel. I felt as if they expected me to join in. Shaun kept catching my eye and looking at me as if he wanted me too. Was he saying join in, or get lost? I couldn't tell. Sometimes the cleft between opposites is small — fascism/communism, love/hate, come here/piss off. If I joined in what would I do? Who would I touch first? Should I kiss Shaun? Then Kath gave me a definite piss off look. Sometimes it's good to be unwanted. I went to bed and pretended to be asleep — my favourite hiding place.

Ross, Virginia and Nerida were gone a long time. My brain kept telling me to sleep, but I fought to stay awake so I could pretend to be asleep when they returned. I needed to be alert, analyse all glances, sentences, gestures, so I'd know where I stood with Virginia.

11.50 pm. When I heard the hum of Ross's well-tuned Valiant pull up outside the shed it actually reminded me of when I used to lie in bed waiting for my father to get home from work. I'd always listen for the sound of his engine, the crunching of his handbrake, then him scraping his dried-out dinner into the fliptop bin. Only when I'd heard this sequence of noises was I convinced Mum and Dad were not breaking up.

'You guys took a while.' (Kath)

'We stopped for sex.' (Nerida)

'Next time I get petrol money.' (Ross)

'Find Danny?' (Kath)

'Na.' (Virginia)

'Where's he gone?' (Kath)

'I don't know, do I.' (Virginia)

'I'm only asking, babe.' (Kath)

'Where's Sandy?' (Virginia)

'Asleep.' (Shaun)

'He'll show up, babe.' (Kath)

Virginia came over to the bed. Oh no! She knows. 'Sandy. Sandy,' she whispered. Each 'Sandy' was like a snowflake, similar but different. Her craft-orientated hands lightly shook my shoulder, but I gritted my teeth and stayed in my deep feigned sleep. I didn't want to be found.

The moment the lights went out the sounds of foreplay commenced on the other side of the partition. A little while later Virginia tumbled down the ravine and joined me on the valley floor. I wondered if Miranda had told her about Terri? I couldn't take any risks. I had to assume she knew. Like a submarine releasing an oil slick in an attempt to confuse the enemy lurking above, I made some sleeping sounds to distract her. If we were going to break up it was going to be in the morning and in a private place. Not here. One minute passed. Two. Three. Was she asleep? I was below periscope depth so I couldn't check. Four minutes passed. The pressure from being in such deep water could crush my hull at any second, but I had to remain locked in silent running mode. Unfortunately, I twitched to stop a pain in my shoulder and that's all it took to blow my cover — one bloody twitch. Virginia's sonar located life in my slumbering eastern European vessel. Her craft-orientated hand touched my ribcage and stomach. Two fingers formed into a little person that promptly marched towards my play area, triggering the first of many depth charges. They say drowning is the most pleasant way to go. It is.

Lights out at 12.35 am.

Tuesday 24 December

Me as a wagtail

Before going to town (Kath's idea: I–I) I sat in a gully filled with trees (about 100 metres from the shed). This is probably what the property looked like before the Greens cleared the land and introduced cattle. I was mesmerised by a family of wagtails — two parents and a mature chick. I thought most infant wagtails would have left the nest by December, but obviously, even in the bird community there are overprotective parents. Or chicks that won't leave home. The wagtail parents looked tired, as they barely kicked up a fuss trying to discourage two hungry myna birds that fancied their chick for lunch. To help the wagtails I imitated the scratching sound they make when they're angry. You've got to admire those myna birds. I looked and sounded like a 90 kilo wagtail and neither of them took a backward step. For twenty minutes in this picturesque gully I was involved in an intense struggle for life. I suspect I was projecting a lot of myself into the wagtails' situation and that's why I was so keen to help them. I was visualising how our neighbours must view my family — two overprotective parents defending an oversized chick reluctant to leave the valley of plenty. And who wouldn't want to stay in this gully of plenty — the gentle trickle of water, glimpses of the black river below and the cool relief from the hot December sun? The only downer was I had to keep moving because there were bull ants about. You can learn a lot about yourself from nature. I learnt that I was overprotected, a tad sentimental and myna birds were not afraid of me.

10.30 am. (Thoughts driving to Iluka with Kath and Shaun.)

I'm not enjoying this holiday as much as I thought I would. Lack of privacy is one factor. Miranda hassling me is another. My back was stiff from helping with the boatshed. Danny's like a bloody hawk circling above me all the time. I'm close to telling Ross to piss off too. I wonder if I could beat Ross in a fight? I reckon I could let Ross hit me three times in the face and still throw a punch that would hurt him more than he'd hurt me. I wonder if he does karate? Mm, maybe if I just let him hit me on the body that would be better. Three hits in the face might be too much.

5.15 pm. (Thoughts during a drive to the Yamba Hotel in Ross's car.)

After seeing the trouble the others were going to, re the eisteddfod, I felt I needed to make a bigger impression at the eisteddfod than 'Alley Cat'. For instance, Kath has spent two days building wooden structures and soaking vast amounts of marine rope in two-stroke petrol. Ross has been collecting bottles and filling them with varying amounts of water. Miranda and Virginia keep disappearing to work on something special. So I started trawling my past for any occasions when I'd made an impression.

Running onto a football field in Armidale, trying to tackle someone who'd made a break, then being palmed off. Pulling my pants down at a wedding. Snapping back and forth on the dance floor at the Leagues Club like I'd been electrocuted during the resident band's penultimate song. The band always finished with a 1970s medley and all the unattractive boys would leave their positions near the fire extinguishers to hit the dance floor. Even the most inhibited men, fuelled by good spirits, would rock from side to side like cats coughing up fur balls. That's what gave me my idea. I'd packed my red cowboy shirt, red rayon trousers and the tiny purple bermudas I'd found on the road near Foster just in case we had a fancy dress night. (I could go as a cowboy or an Italian movie star.) The cowboy shirt had studs instead of buttons, so I knew it'd be easy to take off, and the rayon pants were too big for me, so they would come off easily too. If I danced like I did at the club, but took it a step further, ie strip down to the purple bermudas and pull a pair of underpants out of my shorts and put them on my face, I'd surprise everyone. (I'd seen Tonk, a Norfolk boy, do something similar standing on a snooker table at a pub.) By doing this I'd be saying I'm not afraid to humiliate myself to be remembered. I'm not ashamed of my body. Is that a good or a bad thing?

6.05 pm. Dinner at a Chinese restaurant.

Went to a $4.00 Chinese smorgasbord for dinner. Only one other table was occupied — a family of five celebrating Christmas early. They were seated around a round table with a lazy Susan — a Crowd Pleaser Coke stood in the middle of their table like a silent sentinel. They were freshly showered and wore cheap cardboard party hats that made them appear simple. If I narrowed my eyes it looked as if the ceiling fans that quivered above them were actually trying to make the whole occasion take off, but deep down you knew their helicopter was going nowhere fast. I felt an overwhelming sadness. This family was eating here for real, this was a treat, where-as we were here because Shaun felt it was ironic to eat at such a kitsch place. The family of five ate with their mouths closed, and said please and thankyou whenever they were attended to by the waiter. We were loud, flicked food and swore a lot. However, my impression of this family changed dramatically when they were leaving and I overheard the husband telling his wife, 'It was much better when it was only three dollars instead of four.' The sadness I'd felt for them evaporated — especially when they piled into a Mercedes and roared off without using the blinker.

Rang Mum and Dad from a public phone. I didn't get to speak to Dad — he was in the backyard working on the retaining wall he'd been building for the last ten years. (He'd been going to a beach and bringing back five large rocks in the boot of his car every weekend for ten years. He'd meticulously fit each rock into the wall in a bid to stop our rich topsoil sliding down to the new subdivision below.) So I talked to Mum instead. She told me the weather was foul, but she hoped it was nice where I was. I said it was nice. Then she made me talk to Aunty Coral. Aunty Coral told me the weather was foul down there, but she hoped it was nice up my way. I told her the weather was nice up here, but I'd heard it was foul down her way. Just as Mum got back on the phone to tell me about the weather tomorrow I ran out of coins. I knew they'd be saying, 'Oh well, at least he's rung now and that's the main thing.' Mum would probably stick her head out the back door and tell Dad, 'Sandy phoned.' He'd say, 'Is he having nice weather?' 'Apparently it's lovely up there.' It's nice to be able to speak to your family.

7.39 pm. The pub.

It was good sitting with Shaun and Danny because they were handsome and attracted a lot of attention from holiday-makers and locals alike. Usually when I go out I sit with unattractive types who inevitably finish a night on the local headland drinking beer and hitting a drum kit that one boy carries in the boot of his car. After the pubs shut he sets up the kit, those with cars train their headlights on it and everyone has a turn to whack it. It's amazing how much noise twenty unattractive men can make, especially if a southerly is blowing. It was a pleasant change to sit with guys from further up the food chain.

You have to admire Kath. She insisted on taking her bucket to the pub, plus she wore a cardigan made from a cardboard box. The buttons were actually drawn on in black texta. Funnily enough, the local surfers tried to spit in her bucket just like the Norfolks do at home. No matter where you go, you give a surfer a target and they can't resist it.

Difference between locals and tourists:

Local boys had bleached hair and didn't tuck their shirts in. Local women wore sarongs and sandals. Tourists seemed more manicured, wore smart/casual clothes and they had holiday tans, or recently acquired sunburn. I wore slacks with a cuff, a T-shirt with a zipper and my hair was still wet from the shower. I have thick hair and it takes longer to dry than most people's hair. My hair is so thick you can bounce a Weet Bix off it. I know this because I've done it. Well, I've had it done to me.

Most local boys appeared to be seeking unattended tourist girls to mate with. One cocky local bounced up to Virginia and asked her how she got up here. 'Choo choo.' He did a train motion with his arms. Virginia shook her head. Then he went 'Vroom vroom', making a car shape by miming a steering wheel. Virginia shook her head again. Then he stretched his arms out wide and made a jet sound. Virginia laughed. 'Would you be interested in me sexually or emotionally?' Virginia shook her head. The local surfer with the outline of his sunglasses burnt onto his face went blank for a second, turned to his mates, raised his arms in the air and yelled triumphantly, 'Nineteen knock-backs.' His mates gave him a dull round of applause and then he moved on to another tourist to repeat the same procedure and (I suspect) fail once more. Virginia thought if the locals updated their approach they might have some success because, as she said, 'A lot of them are babes.' Obviously their old ways weren't working any more, but since they couldn't change them and there wasn't much else to celebrate in the local area they picked a failure to mate during the tourist season as the reason to feel good about life. Sometimes celebrating failure can indicate a fear of change.

Nerida was in heaven. Every boy that wobbled past was instantly ranked out of ten. Both Rhys and her were like commentators at a beauty pageant. I joined them for a while as a guest commentator — it was fun thinking about boys as sex objects. That was until it was my turn to go to the bar and they ranked me a four.

The band played mostly 1970s covers: Talking Heads, Marvin Gaye, Neil Young. I didn't dance myself. Shaun did. He danced with quite a few different women and I even said to Virginia at one point something like, 'Kath'll be spewing'.

'It turns her on, babe.'

I suddenly flashed back to the previous night when I was sitting at the table watching them kiss.

After the pub closed we wandered about with no particular focus. We looked in a few shops, then rolled down the hill towards the river like a noisy scrum, seeking things to tip over or break. Along the way we met two other scrums who wished us a merry Christmas.

11.50 pm. In Shaun's car with Kath and Virginia.

It's a long drive from Yamba to Iluka. It's just across the river as the crow flies — a powerful throwing arm could almost skip a flat stone across the channel — but it's half an hour in a car, or eighteen minutes in Shaun's car. Shaun is twelve minutes faster than everybody else.

As we drove along Virginia rested her head on the back of the seat (if I do that I vomit), staring up into the night sky through the back window.

'No moon,' she exhaled.

'Prawns would be running,' said Shaun in a mock yobbo voice. I wasn't interested in prawns. I was feeling claustrophobic in the back seat of his Datsun 120Y. It was this two-door car thing. I knew I couldn't get out of the car unless Kath or Shaun let me. I like to have my own door when I'm in another person's car. Two-door cars are undemocratic.

'We should get some seafood for tomorrow,' said Shaun as he drove with just two fingers resting on the wheel. 'You guys want any oysters?' Kath said 'Yes', Virginia said 'Yes' and I agreed with them so I'd be in the majority.

12.28 am. At the end of a narrow track on the outskirts of Iluka we parked behind a bush and walked towards the salty smell of the black river. I followed the others like a worried pilot fish. I wanted to ask what we were doing, but I was too afraid I was missing the obvious and if I said anything everyone would 'der' me. So I shut up and followed. I knew if I left my host (Shaun) for too long I'd get isolated. Unless the pilot fish is attached to a host it has no identity. Its whole reason to be is to find a larger, more confident host to use for personal gain. However, I wasn't convinced my host had my best interests at heart. Where was this bloody shop that sold oysters after midnight anyway? Suddenly Shaun stopped walking and looked down at this tiny rowboat that was sitting in front of us on the shell-encrusted beach. 'Bingo,' he said.

'Where are the oysters then?' I asked, hiding a mixture of panic and anger.

'Out there, man ... Out there.'

When I realised there was no shop and we were going to steal oysters from a lease I tried to act calm. 'Oyster leases are fiercely guarded.'

Shaun turned on me. He called me gutless. That was his way, belittle others to inflate yourself, and it worked. I simply restuck myself to the reckless host and helped Shaun, Kath and Virginia push the tiny rowboat out onto the river.

'Where are the oars?'

'We don't need oars.' Why no one questioned that I'll never know. It must be a bummer for real pilot fish when they attach themselves to a maverick host because they inadvertently become mavericks themselves and that must go against the grain.

I suppose we were lucky we caught the tide on the turn, otherwise I think Shaun would've been made to look quite stupid. In fact, the ease with which we glided over the dark water in our stolen boat using just our hands to paddle actually made me feel rather secure. It created confidence in Shaun's plan. You could feel a bond growing between us and that in turn created a safety cushion.

'I love oysters kilpatrick,' I said, throwing another imaginary sandbag off my guilty conscience.

'You can have four dozen oysters kilpatrick tomorrow, Sandy.'

I paddled harder when I heard that. I'd always wanted to see if I could eat four dozen oysters kilpatrick in a sitting. It was a dream of mine.

After fifteen minutes of backbreaking work we pulled in alongside a post that said whose oyster lease it was. I was glad it was dark — the more anonymous the crime the less guilt. Virginia, Kath and myself got on one side of the boat to balance it while Shaun reached down into the charcoal water for the oysters. I imagined telling the others about this tomorrow. I'd be in the exclusive oyster club. I wished we each got a special blazer and pennant saying OYSTER CLUB. Shaun got his hand on a pallet but it was too heavy for him to lift out by himself. I wanted to help him, my arms definitely made lifting-like gestures, but my brain was not convinced I was doing the right thing. It was instructing my arms to push the oysters back down. Thankfully the water hid my true intentions. But when Kath joined in, putting her arms around Shaun's waist and pulling him back towards her, and Virginia did the same to me, we started to have success. With four of us working as two couples we managed to get a pallet, covered with hundreds of muddy oysters, up to the side of the boat. Unfortunately (or fortunately), by moving all our resources onto the task of lifting the oysters it meant that no one was holding onto the post, and we started moving off with the now rapidly outgoing tide.

Paddling a tiny rowboat in a strong current using just your arms proved very unrewarding work and we drifted much further down the river than we would have liked, well past the fish co-op and its jetty (our intended landing spot). I started to panic. If someone said the wrong thing to me right then and there I'd have cried, or at least scratched them on the face. Shaun appeared to relish the situation, but his father had the money to bail him out of trouble, or bring him back from the dead if he had to. My father only had a shovel, a mattock and a hammer. He could bury me with those tools but he certainly couldn't bring me back to life.

With a mixture of luck, desperation and Shaun's confidence we made it onto this little sandy beach that clung to a bend in the

seawall. If we hadn't landed there we would have been swept into the surf. Just as well we didn't have any oysters with us because there were quite a few fishermen about and we would have looked suss at 2.00 am in a boat without oars and a pallet full of oysters. When you go into the unknown sometimes it's better to come back empty-handed.

Wednesday 25 December (Christmas Day)

Woke up early — a hold over from the days when I used to wake up at dawn to get the disappointment of Christmas over with quickly. This was my first Christmas away from home. No parents, no large boxes wrapped to hide small boxes hiding a cheap microscope, a plastic PA system, or a glider that would only last till night-time, before it broke. I pictured my family sitting by the phone waiting for me to ring. 'He hasn't rung yet. Maybe all the lines are busy with other people ringing home for Christmas?' Virginia was still asleep down in the valley. A bed was squeaking on the other side of the partition. Surely Shaun and Kath weren't still going from last night? I was starving, but if I got up and made myself something to eat the others would ask me to make them something to eat as well. I'd never made anyone else something to eat before. So I stayed in my bed, hungry, guilty, thinking of home and sharing the familiar sex sounds of Kath and Shaun.

10.00 am. Ross and Nerida had started to prepare Christmas dinner.

Before Ross got too absorbed I asked about borrowing some music for the dance I was doing in the eisteddfod. (He had a vast CD collection in his car.)

'You're leaving it a bit late?' Shut up prick, I thought, but because I wanted something from him I remained civil — the Real Estate training was really coming in handy again. I must admit, Ross was likeable when he was more knowledgeable about something than you. So I explained my idea using as much self-deprecation as I could. He suggested (among other things), Sam Butera playing 'Night Train'. I had no idea who Sam Butera was and I'd never heard of the song 'Night Train', but after a few listens in the Valiant I was relieved to find it actually suited my needs perfectly. (It was striptease music.) The only sacrifice I had to make for borrowing the CD was listening to Ross tell the complete Sam Butera story.

11.48 am. The smell of Christmas dinner was literally driving me insane. The insides of my stomach felt orange. I was like a hungry shark patrolling the area nearest the stove, hoping something would fall out of the oven and I could gobble it up. To take my mind off food I sat in Shaun's car and listened to 'Night Train' a few times, going through some moves I might use in my dance. I was unsure whether to strip right off or stay in the purple bermudas. I didn't want to offend anyone, but I wanted to be remembered. Is it possible to be remembered without offending? *(NB Another possible after-dinner discussion.)*

12.20 pm. Virginia asked me to go for a walk. I thought, Oh oh, this is serious. She was acting strange, like she didn't want the others to know we were sneaking off. I thought, Here we go, here was that talk about Terri. That's why, when we walked through the paspalum towards the river, thumping the ground in front of us to scare off any snakes (no one told me there were snakes), I sorted through some explanations I could use, hoping to find one that made it look as if she was in the wrong. However, before I was prepared Virginia stopped walking, lay down on the grass and stared blankly up into the sky. I did the same because I felt stupid standing next to her with nothing to do. So we both lay on this grassy hill overlooking the black river without speaking — two unsettled people in an enormous double bed waiting to be taken somewhere better. I guess she was acting weird because she was about to tell me something traumatic. I was acting weird because I was about to be told something traumatic. That hawk was circling above us too, like a drunk man trying to remove a KICK ME sign from his back.

Then Virginia touched my arm. Not the touch of someone who was angry, more the touch of a desperate person. Instinctively, when I'm touched lightly lust shoots through my body. Whether lust was the appropriate emotion I don't know, but it certainly gave me some unexpected charm. I rolled towards her for a kiss but she moved and I missed her lips, catching her on the shoulder instead. I quickly made it look as if I meant to kiss her on the shoulder by kissing her shoulder again.

'What are you doing, babe?'

'Kissing your shoulder.'

I'd obviously picked the wrong emotion. (There's more to relationships than sex.) The hawk was still above us, its wings quivering in anticipation of a fresh carcass I suspect. They say a hawk can read a book from 100 feet away. They don't understand anything, but they can see the print. Sounds like Year 11.

'There's something I want to say.'

(Here it comes.)

(Faithful re-creation of actual dialogue.)

'About Danny.'

'You want to get back together.' *(I seized the initiative.)* 'You want to get back with Danny. I know.'

'Is that what you think? Is it? I asked him up here to get back with him?'

(Emergency. Go to Plan B. Tell her about Terri.)

'I love you, babe.'

(I quickly reciprocated.) 'I love you too.'

'I know you do, babe.'

(Wow! An unexpected chance to say 'I love you' and then have it confirmed. I'd feared saying 'I love you' to Virginia in case it wasn't reciprocated. That has got to be the emptiest feeling in the world, when you tell your partner you love them and they don't reciprocate. I fear that fall. On the other hand when a partner says I love you first you've got a safety net, you're suddenly full of confidence, all you have to do is reciprocate, or not reciprocate, so I reciprocated. It was a weight off my mind, not only to hear it said, but to say it back. But as usual I was an idiot because I didn't have to ask the next question, but I did.)

'Too much?'

'What?'

'Do I love you too much?'

'Sometimes.'

(I knew it. Shit. She thinks I'm overbearing. Shit.)

'Danny is in deep shit, babe.'

(An unexpected twist.)

'He collected this money for Snake's twenty-first. You know Snake?'

(I was still thinking about the love thing.)

'You know Snake?'

'What? Yes. Snake!' *(How could I forget Snake. He stuck me on a clothes line once while two other boys filled my pants with coleslaw.)*

'Danny collected this money, right. For Snake's birthday, right. Over one thousand bucks from the boys at the beach. But because he's got this debt he went to the illegal casino, right. You know the one above the Vienna Restaurant?'

'Right.' (*NB I'm at my funniest when I have no expression on my face and my delivery is flat.*)

'He thought he could use the money to make some money and pay back these other dudes he owes money to for something else, but he blew it playing roulette. They serve metho with Coke when you're betting — he got pissed and blew it. If he doesn't show up with a stereo for Snake next Saturday they're gunna kill him. These other dudes are gunna kill him too. He asked me but I haven't got a thousand bucks.'

(*I didn't really know what to do. I was expecting to break up. I imagined what my father would say.*)

'What about his parents?'

'They've got nothing.'

(*I even adopted the tone my father used when he was trying to solve a family problem.*)

'Your parents?' (*After all, Virginia only pretended to be poor — middle class poverty.*)

'I can't ask my father.'

'Who are these dudes anyway? Do I know them?'

'They're heavy dudes.'

'How heavy?'

'Heavy.'

'Kill heavy, or beat up heavy?'

'How would I know, babe? What about you? Can you lend him the money? You got a thousand?'

'Twelve hundred actually.' (*What a stupid time to be competitive, bragging about having more money than Danny.*) 'I can't remember my pin number.'

'It's cool if you don't want to, but if you can that would be beautiful.'

'Ask Shaun.'

'He knows the guys Danny's ripped off.'

'Does Danny know I know?'

'I told him you'd help out.'

'Oh.'

'He wasn't sure about you, but I told him you were cool.'

(Expectation — my least favourite thing. At least I knew why she'd been acting strange and I knew why Danny was here. He didn't want to be found.)

'It's not my money to lend. It's my parents' money.'

'If you can't that's cool. Don't worry, babe.'

'What's he gunna do?'

'There's another way. But you can't tell the others.'

'What?'

'You can't say anything.'

'Okay.'

'He's cased out this surf shop.'

'What?'

'For us to rob. All you have to do is drive the car. It's cool. You don't have to go in the shop, you drive the car. You're not really involved.'

(What in the hell was she talking about?)

'I can't drive a manual.'

'We'll hire an automatic. Come on. He's in deep shit, babe. Come on. We're only taking jeans. We'll drive up to the Gold Coast, sell what we can at some of the beaches and come back. It's almost too easy.'

(Why was she so keen to commit a robbery to help someone who'd ripped off his friends? Did she feel guilty about dropping him? Was it cool for her to be acting poor? Had Danny sucked her in? Perhaps she genuinely felt she was doing a good deed? When I was sitting behind my imitation wood desk, staring through my bushy fringe as the sun

passed over the gap between Grace Bros and David Jones, I never visu-
alised robbing a surf shop on my holidays. I pictured domestic chores,
kissing when the lights were low, talking confidentially by the fire. I
even saw an Afghan dog running into the breeze and some sexy pillow
talk after intimacy, but not robbery.)

1.30 pm. Christmas dinner: prawn cocktails, roast chicken, baked
potatoes, beans, pumpkin and gravy. A complex lunch.

Shaun made the prawn cocktails. I think the reason he made
them was to create a springboard for him to tell the oyster raid
story. It was nice to be a main character in an exciting story as told
by a charismatic person. I liked the cocktail sauce on the prawns
too. Salty and tangy. The prawns combined with the oyster story
was easily my favourite repast so far. Although I'd have to say there
were quite a lot of things going on underneath this menu that
retarded my enjoyment of the meal. Sitting on one side of me was
Miranda, the other side was Rhys, Danny was opposite, next to him
Virginia. I was surrounded by well-established problems. And as if
that wasn't enough, I could see Kath's makeshift eisteddfod stage
waiting to humiliate me. Everywhere I looked there was expectation.
The only positive thing was since Virginia shared the burden of
Danny's dilemma some of her natural joy had returned. To balance
that out, I'd lost some of mine. It was a complex lunch.

For dessert we had boiled fruit cake and custard with liqueur.
Custard should never have a liqueur in it. Sweets are sweets
because they're meant to be sweet.

7.00 pm. Eisteddfod

Thankfully I wasn't first on. Rhys had that honour, followed by Miranda and Virginia, Shaun, me, an interval of ten minutes to set up Ross's bottles, Nerida, Ross's actual performance, then Kathy's fire sculptures to finish.

Act One: Rhys 'The First Lady'

A large brown box (with the word Westinghouse crossed out and Greek Islands written over the top of it) was in the middle of the stage. From where I sat (the second row) it appeared to be full of newspapers, but I wasn't sure. We waited in silence for about 30 seconds — Virginia, Miranda, Nerida, Ross, Shaun, Danny, Owen, Tina and myself — glancing at each other, rolling our eyes at the delay, when suddenly, from out of nowhere, two hands in black gloves appeared from within the box, like gladioli blossoming in a time lapse film. Loud disco music started playing, causing a mound of black hair to slowly rise up from inside the box. When the eyes (fenced in by false eyelashes) were about level with the top of the box, they snapped open. It was Rhys made up like a woman. He started lip syncing to the disco song I didn't recognise. Miranda squealed, 'It's Jackie O! It's Jackie O!' and everyone laughed and clapped. At first I was more absorbed by practicalities, ie how could he get out of such a tall box without falling forward? No sooner had I worried about that than Rhys's arms dropped inside the box, a shiny blade broke through the cardboard and began tearing upwards, causing newspapers and himself (wearing a full-length dress) to spew out. Without skipping a word Rhys unfolded to his/her full glory, moving his hips from side to side in time with the disco music. For about a minute he did the same sideways movement adding little suggestive hand movements to emphasise extra meaning in certain lyrics. It was mesmerising, funny and different. I loved it. Then, just as it seemed he could go on forever, the music stopped and it was over. The only theatre I'd seen before this was *Calamity Jane* by the Acaridans, so it was quite an eye-opener for me. However, there was one more surprise. While everyone applauded Rhys casually turned around and revealed that his dress had been specially altered to show his hairless buttocks. (My buttocks are so hairy.) Rhys's dance was funny. It was like his insides were on the outside.

Act Two: Miranda and Virginia 'Time Line'

Miranda and Virginia stretched a long piece of twine across the stage. When it was fully extended and taut, like a tuned guitar string, Virginia stuck little yellow squares of paper (each square had a number from I to I0 written on it) to the twine at regular intervals. Then Miranda and Virginia took up their starting positions on either side of the stage, approximately four metres apart and waited. Classical music started (I knew from the movie *Ten* with Bo Derek that it was *Bolero*), and they placed the twine in their mouths and slowly ate their way towards each other (like the dogs in *Lady and the Tramp*), keeping their hands behind their backs, holding the twine with their teeth and storing the consumed twine in their cheeks. Whenever they reached a yellow square they removed it with their hands and stuck it on their faces. It seemed very flat. A good idea on paper, but in reality it didn't work. It was funny when they got the giggles because with their mouths so full of twine it was difficult to keep the string taut and breathe at the same time, but I'm afraid that was the only highlight for me. *(NB Apparently the squares with numbers represented the amount of months they'd been friends.)*

Act Three: Shaun 'The Mock Race Call'

I didn't see Shaun's act because I was inside the shed getting ready for my act. Instead of a poem as he originally intended he did a mock race call. Apparently Kath took an old form guide, picked out a horse race and sold the individual horses to those who could afford to buy one for ten dollars. Once all the horses were sold Shaun returned from where he was hiding (he didn't know who had bought what horse) and called the race using a mock yobbo voice and an empty beer glass as a microphone. The winning owner (Owen) received all the money. I was so nervous I couldn't listen to him. I was like the last Tasmanian tiger walking nervously around the confines of his small cage. All I knew was when I heard the applause for Shaun it was not long until I was on.

Act Four: Sandy 'Dance'

Suddenly 'Night Train' started. I stuck my arm around the edge of the backdrop and wiped it up and down the oily tarpaulin until I got a reaction. I was so nervous my fingers tingled and my head felt light, but thankfully as I jumped out in front of my fellow holiday-makers, dressed head to toe in a red nylon cowboy outfit, my tanks instantly filled with confidence. Confidence is such a funny thing because the moment I had it I did something unexpected, ie I licked the tarpaulin before walking towards centre stage (as planned) to the grinding sound of Sam Butera, making little pelvic thrusts as I went. (I didn't expect to do that.) In fact I was so full of confidence that when I got centre stage I paused a second and inhaled — the attention smelt so good, like a thousand rissoles coated in my mother's gravy. Catching Danny's eye threw me for a bit, but when I wiped my hands over my body like a sexy man might do and undid the first of the five studs on my red cowboy shirt Danny's shadow faded away.

After undoing three studs I became impatient and tore my shirt open, slipped it off and twirled it over my head like a drunken PE student. Huge cheer. I was performing with the skill of a pro here. There were a series of stops in the music where I'd planned to thread my shirt between my legs and do a sawing motion, but due to my earlier indulgences, ie licking the tarpaulin and inhaling attention, I missed them. To cover I turned side on and pushed my stomach out to make it seem as if I had a huge tan paunch. But I still found myself in front of the music, so I faced the tarpaulin and playfully touched a small patch of wiry hair at the base of my spine.

Everything unexpected was funny. Once the music caught up with me and I was back on track I slowly slid the red pants down my fleshy legs. They temporarily caught on my desert boots, but my panicked efforts to free them only made everyone laugh even more. I turned front on, my 90 kilo frame snugly contained in the tiny bermudas. I wet my index fingers and ran them around my nipples like two motorbikes riding the wall of death at the annual agricultural show. If only the Tasmanian tiger could have done what I was doing then maybe things would have been different. Then I spread my arms like Jesus and thrust my pelvis in and out like an excited horse in spring. Everything loose wobbled. I reached into my pants, grabbed the Y-fronts I'd set in front of my real undies and teased them out, little by little, licking my lips and rolling my eyes as if I were a crazy man. Then I held the undies up in the air like a lucky dip, wiped my armpits/bottom and put them over my head so I could stick my dry tongue through the Y-hole before throwing them onto the floor for the big finale. Sadly, I mistimed the dive onto the undies and landed on my elbow, but because I was so drunk on limelight I didn't feel it. I flipped over and over on the undies like a dog after a bath. Then (not a moment too soon) the music finished and the sweet mist of extreme success engulfed me as I lay on the stage, gasping for air like a dying fish.

It was only when I departed the limelight that the pain from the mistimed dive established itself. I suppose there is a certain amount of pain involved in exposing yourself.

Act Five: Nerida 'Sex Lesson'

I got back at the end of Nerida's sex lesson. All I saw was a drawing of two people in a sexual embrace. Above it were the words 'Position No. 20: No sweat technique. Both partners lie still and don't move.' Based on the little I saw I would have liked to have seen the whole thing.

Act Six: Ross 'Bottles'

Ross had set twenty bottles all filled with varying amounts of water on a table placed centre stage. Unfortunately, as Kath introduced him she made this large sweeping hand gesture that tipped her off balance and she stumbled onto the table, knocking every single bottle off. The expression on Ross's face was priceless. It was as if a timber jigger had wiped out his entire family. No one could stop themselves from laughing. We pretended to console him, but deep down we were laughing inside long after the broken glass had been cleared away. It was devastating for him, but so funny for us. Sympathy didn't come easily to Kath and forgiveness was not Ross's greatest asset, so it was rather interesting to watch their reconciliation.

Act Seven: Kath 'Fire Walk with Me'

Eventually our attention was diverted to five wooden structures placed five metres apart, all covered in the same thick marine rope. They looked like messy Mexican statues and from where I sat all you could smell was petrol. It was as if someone was mowing lawn close by. Kath lit a torch, raised it above her head, then, like a solid-looking elf with a big smile, she pranced daintily between the wooden structures lighting the rope. I suspect the rope was meant to burn in such a way it would illuminate the intricate patterns she'd created. I think the rope (soaked through with gasoline), burnt far more furiously than anyone could have imagined, and what's more, it gave off dense black clouds of toxic smoke as well. So we couldn't see anything and we had to run because everyone experienced severe breathing difficulties. Kath certainly got the biggest reaction, but deep down we knew it had gone terribly wrong. You may be able to control a social scene with the force of your personality Kath, but when you play with fire things can go terribly wrong.

The only negative comment about my contribution was from Miranda. She said she felt embarrassed watching me. She said she found what I did sad, repulsive and blokey. I wonder if the others felt the same. I thought everyone loved what I did.

Lights out just after midnight. The eisteddfod had distracted me from thinking about the robbery, but as I lay there trying to sleep I felt haunted by what was expected of me. Should I do it? Or should I not do it? They are the questions. If I did it what would be the positives? Virginia would be happy. Danny would be grateful. I would be in another club — the I-drove-the-getaway-car-in-a-robbery club. *(See page 154.)* I would be helping someone who was less fortunate than me. The negatives? I could get caught. I would freeze under pressure. I'd been into the surf shop and seen the owner. In fact, he had been helpful. I pictured the Norfolks taking the wheels off my Gemini and putting it up on bricks after they found out I'd helped Danny rip them off. I pictured them stealing my board shorts, stuffing dog turds in the pockets, burying them in sand and saying, 'Your shorts are over there, Sandy. Eh Sandy, lend us two bucks. Ah sucked in ... Scab.' I think the negatives had it.

Shit! I forgot to ring Mum and Dad for Christmas.

Thursday 26 December

9.40 am. Danny picked us up

The plan was to drive to Byron Bay and hire the automatic car for me to use in the robbery. I was determined: the moment I got in the car I'd tell them I was not doing it. No way, Jose. I had to be strong. Pull down the roller door, so to speak. Unfortunately, as soon as I plonked myself down in the passenger seat of the Statesman Virginia started rubbing my shoulders. I knew if I said anything she'd stop. I'd waited so long to get a bloody neck rub I wasn't going to let anything get in my way now. And Danny seemed so grateful I'd decided to help him. (I hadn't said I would, but unable to say yes obviously means yes.) So I thought, I'll just absorb a few side benefits from being a good helper then I'll tell them I'm out.

10.00 am. Danny smiled. I think he laughed too, but he disguised it by putting a hand over his mouth. I couldn't be absolutely sure his lips moved. I never imagined a beautiful man like Danny could be so needy. He'd been a Norfolk since he was thirteen, a close friend of the local surf god Mongrel, he knew Craw (a previous surf god), and here I was, Sandy, the boy with too much hair on one side of his head, sitting next to him, heading towards Byron Bay to help him in a robbery.

Perhaps he didn't know that Virginia had told me about the heavy dudes and the illegal casino already, or perhaps he wanted to tell me about it all himself. Whatever his motives, Danny babbled on and on about the underworld, the Norfolks and his boss. He told me how he and two other guys sat on the roof of a wool store one winter night, waiting (with rifles) to ambush some heavy guys who were trying to rip off his boss. He told me how his boss shot his gun off into the roof of a hotel whenever he was drunk. He told me about Roy (an employee of his boss) who killed people for a thousand bucks. Roy even visited him at his aunt's place recently and he gave Danny a going over because the boss reckoned Danny had his hand in the till. 'He reckoned I took two hundred and fifty bucks.' The way Danny described Roy screaming 'Arh arh' after every punch was absolutely frightening. When he told me this stuff I didn't feel the same bond growing between Danny and me as I'd felt in the tiny rowboat with Shaun on Christmas Eve. I didn't detect a safety cushion forming under me. The oyster club seemed such a nice middle-class crime compared to this one. If both these crimes were cats then the oyster raid was like a domestic cat hunting a bird after it had already eaten a plate of Snappy Tom. Today's crime was feral. Danny had drifted into a very very dark world indeed. I began hoping my eye would puff up so I could say I needed to go to a doctor and get an antibiotic.

Noon. Byron Bay.

How often had I hidden inside my bushy fringe and imagined living in Byron Bay? In my dream I was with Virginia plus a dog. We owned a half-finished place with a verandah, we'd get up early to surf, wander about in thongs, live on fruit salad and spend the money I'd made from doing something special. But as we approached Byron, it was overcast and I was in an old Statesman with two other frightened people and we were organising a robbery. If only I'd paid for my Real Estate books I wouldn't have had $1200 in the bank. I wouldn't feel so guilty about not giving Danny the money. If I gave him the money I wouldn't have to do the robbery.

I realised (at the car rental place) that Virginia and Danny expected me to hire the getaway car using my money. That would be like saying,

'Yes I will drive the car in the robbery.' It meant if we got caught it'd be my name on the form. In some ways I felt quite mature because I was the one taking the responsibility, but after I'd paid the money over and exchanged a few platitudes with the pleasant employee, my good cheer was replaced by full-blown anxiety.

1.45 pm. We all distracted ourselves for an hour by driving around looking for Paul Hogan, but when we didn't see him, or Strop, we headed for home.

I drove the car back to the hobby farm to get used to it. Virginia came with me and Danny drove behind us, so whenever I peered in the rear-view mirror he was there, trailing behind us. To be honest I hoped his car would roll. I didn't want him to be killed or anything, just put in hospital.

8.15 pm. The couples played cards. Virginia and I negotiated some tricky questions about where we were today. We couldn't say anything because Danny didn't want anyone to know about the robbery. It was weird, our whole existence was now controlled by Danny and his bloody robbery. I didn't even want to do it. However, as Shaun's wine took hold of us and the card game turned from five hundred to strip poker, I did say a few things I shouldn't have said. For example: 'I can't cook tomorrow because I'm doing something illegal.' I love the power a secret gives you.

On a positive note, I wasn't the big loser at strip poker. Sure I lost my pants, but never my undies. Ross lost five games in a row and was nude for twenty minutes. Virginia and Nerida were topless for short periods as well. For about an hour I forgot about the robbery and laughed and laughed and laughed.

PS The sex sounds on the other side of the partition didn't belong to Kath and Shaun, but to Ross and Nerida. Kath actually asked them if they could have a night off, so the rest of us could get some sleep. I was disappointed to hear it was them.

I felt people were relating to me differently too. I put that down to the eisteddfod. Or was it because I was preoccupied by what Danny and Virginia expected of me? A few days ago people seemed indifferent to me, now they just seemed unsure. I rate unsure a more effective start to a friendship than indifference. Perhaps being preoccupied made me seem more intelligent.

Lights out at 11.50 pm.

Friday 27 December

11.30 am. Very hot. Went to Iluka beach for a swim. The sand was like the planet Mercury. By the time you ran back from a swim you were hot and if you wanted to cool off you had to run back across the burning sand and start the cycle all over again. On hot days (like today) you could get into a rut at Iluka beach. At least it took my mind off my problems.

12.30 pm. Stopped at the caravan park as Eel Man arrived back carrying his daily sack of eels. If he was in the city dressed in a boiler suit, carrying a sackful of eels, he'd be teased and called crazy. Up here the mere sight of him causes kids to crowd around, begging him for just one look inside his potato sack full of squirming black eels. Even some parents came out of their annexes to have a look. It was like Greg Norman walking up to the 18th, except Eel Man has splayed feet that make him walk like a clown. This was Eel Man's moment of glory, this is why he got up at 5.00 every morning, just so he could walk down the middle of the Woody Head Caravan Park carrying a sackful of eels. It makes you wonder if he used the same eels every day. You'd think if he'd caught six eels a day for the last ten years he'd have cleaned out the eel population in the river three or four times over by now. I suppose there's always a little bit of trickery involved when you're mesmerising people.

2.30 pm. Danny, Virginia, Nerida, Miranda and I went to Yamba.

Danny wanted to walk over the plan for the robbery but because Nerida and Miranda insisted on coming it made it hard for us to talk freely. When Danny wanted to say something about the robbery he used sentences that appeared to say one thing but meant something else. I was glad Nerida and Miranda were there. Not so much Miranda, but any obstacle was a bonus for me.

Nerida was as ebullient as ever. She was wedged in between Miranda and me in the back seat. Our thighs, forearms and shoulders touched. From Chatsworth Island to the Yamba turn-off, a distance of several kilometres, Nerida lay on my lap three times, held my hand (in an ironic way) twice, pretended to style my hair and she also put her hands over Danny's eyes.

When I saw the surf shop I freaked out. I developed my trademark dry cough, my heart sped up and I had this urge to run. A few glances were exchanged and Virginia whisked Nerida and Miranda off to do a grocery shop leaving Danny free to take me through the plan. Why didn't I say something to Danny? Was it because he was a Norfolk? Why was Virginia so into this robbery? Was she simply trying to light up a dark space? Danny and I stood where I'd be parked on the night and he calmly talked me through the robbery. It was like rehearsing loss in advance.

(Rough re-creation of the plan.)

Virginia and Danny break a toilet window at back of shop. Danny climbs in window, opens door for Virginia. Danny fills blanket with jeans while Virginia stands at door as lookout. When Virginia flashes torch twice I move car to front of shop with tailgate down so Danny and Virginia can throw jeans in back and jump in car without double-handling. If there is someone about Sandy flashes lights. If Sandy sees cops he honks horn. If anyone sees us leaving turn lights off so they can't get number plate.

His calmness filled me with confidence, but it didn't give me any hope. The fact he didn't use the word 'the' made the whole thing appear even more unsettling. He suggested we tell the others the three of us were going fishing tomorrow night in order to straighten a few things out. That way no one would question why we were out together.

Saturday 28 December

A 'Loomer'

I had a 'loomer', as my Uncle Nev always called it. When something big was looming on the horizon it was called a 'loomer'. The tension created by this loomer meant I slept like a condemned man and I woke long before my slumber was completed. I just lay in my valley, among the other relics that had fallen into the ravine during the night — coins, socks, a pair of undies I'd half taken off. Virginia was sleeping peacefully beside me. How could she sleep? Was she made of stone?

For once the sex noises had stopped and there was just an eerie calm — except for the hissing sound the toilet made. I remembered a milkman once told my mother that before an earthquake there's always a hissing sound. My only other foray into crime (apart from the oysters) was when Nils and I stole some copper from an old foundry in our suburb. But that project was doomed because when you're thirteen you don't have the business contacts to move a large quantity of stolen copper in a hurry.

I peered at my overnight bag down beside the bed. Things were spewing out of it as if it was bilious, or was there something scary inside it and my clothes were trying to escape? I could probably throw everything into it without too much fuss, sneak outside, carry it down the track and hide it in some bushes. Then I could probably run to the caravan park and grab the car (I had the keys) in less than an hour. I could probably pick up the bag and drive home. It was my car. I was mobile. So I lay there, shifting between the good fortune of realising I could escape and the consequences of leaving behind people relying on me. My family have always been runners and hiders, so genetically speaking I guess my decision was already made for me. I would act on instinct. I'd get out of the cooking too.

(Here's the note I left for Virginia.)

Dear Ginny,

Sorry I had to go so abruptly. In the circumstances I think it is better that I leave while I can. I still love you and I hope you still love me too.

PS Danny is nice. I can see how you found him attractive. I think once he fights some personal demons he'll be a very pleasant chap.

And I left her a poem.

Do you still have the stars in your eyes?
Do you still wear my leather ring?
Do you still sing our favourite song?
I still say your first name whenever I can.

My dear Virginia.
Please don't show this letter to anyone. (Only Nerida.) Please for-give me and please ring me when you get back.
*   Love forever, Sandy.*

(I hoped this letter would go off like a little emotional landmine. What happens if Shaun finds it first and reads it out loud? Damn, it's so hard to be manipulative.)

10.00 am. At the Grafton turn-off I had a cry.

Felt so overwhelmed by guilt it just poured out. Normally I only cry when I see people on television overcoming enormous odds, or in animal pictures.

I'd wondered about the end, what it would feel like. Well ... it felt like being chased by hot lava, but luckily I had a modern car and I was outrunning it. Damn! I'd never know what was built on the concrete slab laid by Kath's dad.

I should have asked Virginia to come with me. Maybe she didn't want to do the robbery either? Although me running away may have saved her? They couldn't do the robbery without me.

I guess I'd have to rethink the rest of my life now because whenever I spent time under my fringe I always imagined Virginia with me. I'd have to lower the pedestal, have it cleaned ready for something else to go up there.

Saw two billboards advertising food. The first one, advertising dairy produce, got me thinking about food. The painting of a just cooked chicken made me really hungry.

Grafton to Coffs.

Played my country tape (it had a few of my other favourite songs on it too) and sang along. I have quite a good voice in the car, it's easy to find harmonies and remember melody lines. I had a bit of spit caught in my throat so I was able to make two notes at once — like a Mongolian throat singer.

I played the following songs in between Grafton and Coffs: 'To

Know Him' by the Teddy Bears, 'Makin Believe' by Kitty Wells, 'Shelter of Your Arms' by Willie Nelson, 'White Rose of Athens' by Nana Mouskouri, 'Sounds of Silence' and 'The Boxer' by Simon and Garfunkel. During 'White Rose of Athens' I got very vivid pictures indeed. Weird things, like the time my parents drove to Goulburn to watch me be a reserve in a rugby league team. I was so glad they came because Mum brought cold chicken and potatoes. The other boys only had chicken-flavoured chips and Pepsi for lunch.

12.20 pm. Coffs to Kempsey.

Stopped at a diner and ate a salty hamburger.

Kempsey to Taree.

On the way up the coast (even though I was asleep for much of the way) you see the ocean more than you do on the way home. The road up leads your eye towards the sea. On the way south, you look at the other side of the road more — the mountains, shredded tyres, bits of paper you threw out on the way up and when you see them again you think, I wonder what brainless twit threw all that rubbish out?

Taree to Raymond Terrace.

Since I was farting so much I decided to keep count. Seventy-five farts between Taree and Raymond Terrace. You could probably add another twenty because I'd already done a few before I started counting. It certainly distracted me. Listened to 'The Lonely Sea' by the Fantastic Baggys, Violent Femmes, Irish folk music and Iron Maiden doing 'Run to the Hills'.

5.30 pm. Home town.

There's something comforting about driving down the mountain that made it so hard to leave, but so easy to return. You could literally turn the engine off and roll into my home town. I suppose if I'd bought the textbooks (like I was supposed to) I wouldn't have been able to hire this car and I wouldn't have been able to escape.

The car hire place was closed by the time I arrived. I had to find some charm so I didn't pay the extra day's hire. If I didn't have a huge desire to be loved I wouldn't have been as charming and I wouldn't have been able to get out of paying the extra costs.

I didn't want to go home just yet. I didn't want to talk to my parents about why I was home early, or how the holiday was, or why I left without asking properly. I didn't really want to be home at all, so I sat in a picnic hut at the north end of my local beach. I often sat there when I was feeling sorry for myself. To kill time I made a final premiership table of friends. Here it is.

1   Virginia. I think guilt was playing a part in keeping her at the number one spot.
2   Nerida. I was attracted to her.
3   Rhys. He never said anything to Virginia about Terri (and he's funny).
4   Ross. His position is more a reflection on how others have sunk.
5   Kath. She'd said I was funny.
6   Danny. I felt sorry for him.
7   Shaun. I didn't like him at all, but he included me in the oyster story and for that I am grateful.
8   Miranda. We just didn't click. I admire her loyalty but ... Actually, I should move her up a few spots because if she defended me like she did with Virginia that would be good.

I sat in the picnic hut for hours. It was useful. I got to write about today plus read back through some of the other days in the journal as well. To be honest, I had to spice them up. Some days were exactly the same. The same things happened at the same time and the same

people tended to say the same things. I tended to use the same tone and the same words, but I suppose this journal is not meant for other people so it doesn't really matter if it's boring. So I've added a few things to make the holiday seem more interesting. You could say not everything in this journal happened. Some of it did, but most of it I made up. I thought I'd seem more complex if my journal appeared to be confessional and real. The other thing I must say is I wrote the ending in advance. Instead of waiting for the rest of today to finish, I just made it up. I was bored sitting in the picnic hut doing nothing, waiting till it was late enough to go home, so I thought I might as well finish today while I had the time to do it. In reality the journal ends now, with me sitting in a picnic hut at the northern end of the local beach. It's 8.33 pm. From where I'm sitting I can see an oval, a tall green fence, some Norfolk pines. To my right there's a seesaw, a swing and I can hear the surf, but I can't see it. If I got up and walked twenty metres east I'd see it, but not from where I am now.

It was after 11.30 pm when I left the picnic hut. I would have stayed there longer except a ranger moved me on. He pretended not to know me, but he did know me because I used to do swimming training with his daughter. Some people take their jobs too seriously. I suppose I was only ten when he knew me and faces can distend quite dramatically between the ages of ten and nineteen.

I walked along the path that ran parallel to the beach, round the fishing harbour, round the bottom corner of the main street where the hoons poured oil onto the road every Thursday night. They hid in the bushes and watched families coming into town spin out. Nice suburban folk would find out if Dad was half the driver he always bragged he was. Tonight there were no hoons. The corner was deserted. I walked up the mall. A car full of unattractive men cruised along looking for pedestrians to hit with the water from their windscreen washers. I was one of those pedestrians. From a distance it looked like their car had glands used specifically for marking out their territory. No point running away from them because they only chased you and that was worse.

At the end of the mall I stopped at the one shop that was open. A smelly takeaway place with flashing lights. This shop never closed. Sometimes I wondered if it really existed, or if it was operated by the walking dead. I ordered a toasted cheese and tomato sandwich. After such an unsettling walk through the mall there was a hole inside me that desperately needed filling. Food usually filled that space for me, or at least chewing something did. The unique thing about this shop was the moment you ordered food it was ready. They made the fastest toasted sandwiches in the world. By the time you ordered, turned and picked up a *TV Week*, your sandwich was ready.

'Toasted tomato and cheese sandwich please.'

'Toasted sandwich ready.'

I stared into the hole I was trying to fill with food. I realised the robbery would be happening now — if it was happening at all, that is. We were meeting in Yamba at 12.15 am. It was 12.15 am now.

What would they be saying about me? Would they hate me? I wonder what they ate for dinner? Once my teeth had ground the hot salty reward into a buttery paste these types of problems went away.

12.45 am. The start of our street was like a breakwater. It was bizarre. Two streets away the wind was so fierce it would remove a wig, in my street it was dead still. I wondered if anything had changed since I was last here just over eight days ago. There were probably five more rocks in our retaining wall. The Gumleys probably had a new car. Mr Price had probably caught some blackfish. I looked towards my house. The outside light was off. They usually left it on. I'd have to dock without navigation. Find my own way into port, so to speak.

As usual the backdoor key was under a piece of soap on the third shelf in our laundry. I opened the back door, returned the key to its hiding place and crept in through the kitchen. Twenty-six dolly steps from back door to hall. Thirty-two dolly steps from hall to my bedroom. Once again my father's snoring drowned out the noisy floorboards near the entrance to the master bedroom. I went quietly past Aunty Coral in the spare room remembering that last time she ambushed me and made me eat. Tonight I made it past without incident. I put my head in the bathroom to say a quick hello to it, then slipped silently on to my room, like a phantom yacht with a cargo of contraband and crew full of secrets. The round trip of the SS puffy eastern European was finally over. My shoulders dropped, my mouth moistened. I was home. I turned on the lamp that sat on the desk I never used any more. Suddenly, like a corpse with muscle tone, the groggy figure of my Aunty Coral sat bolt upright in my bed and stared at me.

'Aunty Coral!' I shrieked. *(She freaked me out.)*

We looked at each other for a second or so, both of us blinking as our eyes adjusted to the light. She seemed embarrassed about

being in my bed. I felt bad that I'd woken
her up, but I was also peeved that
she was in my bed and I couldn't
really ask her to change rooms at
this time of night. When two people
want the same thing usually one
misses out. Would the bed in the
spare room be made up, or would I
have to sleep under a blanket without a
sheet? That would feel prickly on my skin.

    'Arthur?'

'It's Sandy, Aunty Coral.'

'Do you want a steak sandwich, Arthur?'

'It's Sandy.'

'Come on, I'll make you a steak sandwich.'

'I'm not hungry.'

'Come on.'

'I don't want a steak sandwich.'

'Come on.'

'Okay.'

The Shed Intro E

Ev-'ry sum-mer we'd head up north, we'd stay at Kath-y's farm. All the cou-ples stay in the shed the sing-les in the cara-van park. From the shed we'd help Kath's dad work a-round the farm. How'd talk and talk a-bout— it all the diff-'rent pad-docks their diff-'rent charms. Then at night when the fires a-glow you'd get con-fid-ent-ial and you'd talk so low you'd kiss by the can-dle light an hour or so oh 'cause all the sweet-hearts sleep in the shed hol-i-day style, and all the sin-gles fend for them-selves hol-i-day time.

The Shed

Every summer we head up north,
We'd stay at Kathy's farm.
All the couples stay in the shed,
The singles in the caravan park.

From the shed we'd help Kath's dad
Work around the farm.
He'd talk and talk about it all,
The different paddocks, their different charms.

Then at night when the fire's aglow,
You'd get confidential and you'd talk so low.
You'd kiss by the candlelight an hour or so.

'Cause all the sweethearts sleep in the shed holiday style,
And all the singles fend for themselves, holiday time.

But this year seems a little strange,
Things are not the same.
She is keen on someone else.
I've seen her wash his car.
And I am flattered by someone's unexpected charms.
Curious for a minute to be in another's arms.

You can imagine how I screamed driving in the car,
Through the fruit gates' token search down from Yamba.
No more secret motel nights at Nambucca Heads.
I'll never know what's built upon the concrete laid by Kath's dad.

Don't tell her dad because that'd mess it up.
I'd have to stay at the caravan park,
And drive back to Sydney alone in my car.

Alley Cat.

Alley Cat

Alley cat,
Box head toughie,
You're rather scruffy,
Don't you run away from me.
Alley cat, manners so deplorable,
Still you're adorable,
I love you oh don't you see?

Alley, alley, alley, alley cat (meow).
Alley, alley, alley, alley cat (meow)
Alley, alley, 'A' double 'L', 'E', 'Y' are you?
Leaping over fences,
Using all your senses,
Eyeing off affection.
You're discarded and fluffy.
You're discarded and fluffy.
No! Discarded and scruffy.
You're a real cool 'Le chat' Mr Alley Cat.
As they say in France!

Fifty Bucks

Sit-ting in a car   in the   dark in a lane

wait-ing for the torch   wait-ing for the torch-light

sig-nal   to   start up the car   move it up a bit   inch it up, inch it up

inch it up lit-tle by lit-tle   I'll flash my lights   (flash my lights) if

things get hot   (things get hot) I'll honk the horn   (honk the horn)

that means cops   (Cops! Cops!) I've got to help the others in-side the shop

that's my job   CHORUS Two of my friends gave me

fifty bucks   to drive a car in this rob-ber-y   (I)
last time

didn't want to do it, I did-n't have to do it, I didn't need the money I'm

mid-dle class   I just want   (he just wants) ap-pro-val, ap-prov-al, ap-

-prov-al, ap-prov - al   Ap-prov-al!

154

Fifty Bucks

Sitting in a car in the dark in a lane.
Waiting for the torch, waiting for the torch light signal
To start up the car, move it up a bit,
Inch it up, inch it up, inch it up little by little.
I'll flash my lights if things get hot.
I'll honk the horn, that means cops.
I've got to help the others inside the shop.
That's my job.

Two of my friends gave me fifty bucks
to drive a car in this robbery.
I didn't want to do it,
I didn't have to do it,
I didn't need the money, I'm middle class.
I just want approval, approval, approval, approval.
Approval!

There's Danny now and there's the lights,
So I'll grab the jeans, put 'em in a sack and get 'em in the car.
Drive up the Gold Coast,
Sell the jeans at the beach.
That's my job, or so it seems.

My Chocolate Romance

I would go in rain and sun as well. I could park a block a-wa-

some-times two. I could take an hour to pro-per-ly choose the

right sweet for you—. I knew the shop own-er

and his wife well. They'd stop, laugh nev-er try to sell

I just hoped that the sweet I'd bought would last the long way hom

In— my— choc'-late ro-mance—

wrapped in sil-ver pa-per and bound by a blue sash

My Chocolate Romance

I would go in rain and sun as well.
I could park a block away sometimes two.
I could take an hour to properly choose
The right sweet for you.

I knew the shop owner and his wife well,
They'd stop, laugh, never try to sell.
I just hoped that the sweet I'd bought,
Would last the long way home.

I'd pick you up on Thursdays outside your work,
I didn't mind if you'd stayed back to chat.
I'd kiss your lips and we'd talk about your day,
Drive you home the longest way.
In my choc'late romance,
Wrapped in silver paper and bound by a blue sash.

Now I just double park, race in and choose,
I'll buy the first thing that I see.
I'll even buy those yellow things,
From under the bain-marie.

I get so morose when I wait in the car,
I storm down the hall to find where you are.
I'll peck you on the cheek and chat about my day,
Drive you home the quickest way.
In my choc'late romance,
Wrapped in silver paper and bound by a blue sash.

The shop and the owner have long gone away,
No more sweets in a cabinet on display.
They sell hot rolls with cheese spray,
A little pile of chocolates near a cigarette tray.

Acknowledgments

The author would like to thank the following mixture of colleagues, citizens, and acquaintances for their help in producing this journal:

Mikey Robins, Jen Oldershaw, Mark Kennedy, Angela Moore, Anna McAllan, Glenn Butcher (for the sheet music), the frienly staff at JJJ, all surfers in the Angourie/Yamba region of New South Wales and Michael Bell for his expert drawings.